AF606925

VFX still.

THE ART OF

THOR™
THE DARK WORLD

Written by **MARIE JAVINS & STUART MOORE**

Book design by **JEFF POWELL**

Foreword by **CHARLIE WEN**

Afterword by **CHARLES WOOD**

Front cover art by **JOOLS FAIERS**

TITAN BOOKS

FOR MARVEL PUBLISHING
JEFF YOUNGQUIST, Editor
SARAH SINGER, Editor, Special Projects
JEREMY WEST, Manager, Licensed Publishing
SVEN LARSEN, VP, Licensed Publishing
DAVID GABRIEL, SVP Print, Sales & Marketing
C.B. CEBULSKI, Editor in Chief

FOR MARVEL STUDIOS 2013
KEVIN FEIGE, President
LOUIS D'ESPOSITO, Co-President
VICTORIA ALONSO, Executive Vice President, Visual Effects
CRAIG KYLE, Senior Vice President, Production & Development
WILL CORONA PILGRIM, Creative Manager, Research & Development
ERIC HAUSERMAN CARROLL, Creative Executive
MICHAEL ROSS, Senior Vice President, Business & Legal Affairs
RYAN POTTER, Principal Counsel
ERIKA DENTON, Clearances Director
RANDY McGOWAN, VP Technical Operations
ALEX SCHARF, Digital Asset Coordinator
DAVID GRANT, Vice President, Physical Production
ALEXIS AUDITORE, Physical Assets Coordinator

MARVEL STUDIOS' THE INFINITY SAGA -
THOR: THE DARK WORLD: THE ART OF THE MOVIE
ISBN: 9781803365589
E-BOOK ISBN: 9781835411292

First edition: September 2024

10 9 8 7 6 5 4 3 2 1

Published by Titan Books
A division of Titan Publishing Group Ltd
144 Southwark St, London SE1 0UP

www.titanbooks.com

Did you enjoy this book? We love to hear from our readers. Please e-mail us at: readerfeedback@titanemail.com or write to Reader Feedback at the above address.

To receive advance information, news, competitions, and exclusive offers online, please sign up for the Titan newsletter on our website: www.titanbooks.com

A CIP catalogue record for this title is available from the British Library.

Printed and bound in China.

Jackson Sze concept art.

CONTENTS

Charlie Wen keyframe.

My first film with Marvel Studios was *Thor*—so needless to say, the chance to return to Asgard was an opportunity I could not have been more thrilled to embark on. With the first *Thor*, my biggest challenge was finding a way to bring Thor and the inhabitants of Asgard to life. Drawing inspiration from the Jack Kirby comics and the direction of Kevin Feige, Craig Kyle and Director Kenneth Branagh, we forged ahead into crafting an interesting and otherworldly set of personalities. What followed was more than a year of trial and error—finding the right blend of the theatrical and the alien, the regal and the powerful, while still maintaining what made these characters iconic from the comics. More than a year later, we finally found our heroes and with them a foundation of design language for Asgard.

When we started development on *Thor: The Dark World*, Alan Taylor came on the project with a distinct vision that I found equal parts challenging and compelling. He was adamant about finding ways to introduce practical elements as a way to ground these pre-existing characters and make them more tangible. It was a fascinating process to sift through years of ancient history, and numerous intricate design elements and textures, that were only hinted at in the first film. Keeping in mind that Thor and his companions are warriors, I wanted to heavily introduce elements of Norse mythology including leather knot-work and find a way to integrate a sensibility to the costumes, such as straps and fastenings, that would make them understandable at first read. As a designer, I strive to find a way of combining elements to conceive something completely new, even if it contains traces of the pre-existing. This film gave our team the opportunity to do just that.

On the first *Thor*, there were numerous, extremely talented people working simultaneously trying to establish the design language for the film. The only real unification came from the end goal of finding out who these characters were. However, since *Marvel's The Avengers*, the Visual Development team—headed by myself and Ryan Meinerding—has been a hive of camaraderie and creativity for contributing to the films at Marvel Studios. Kevin Feige and Louis D'Esposito have given us the rare opportunity to begin cultivating ideas before true pre-production begins. And in doing that, we have the chance to explore a much wider array of designs and keyframes.

The Visual Development team thrives on artistic collaboration, and this project gave us the opportunity for that on a grand scale. There is a sweeping sense of nostalgia as I flip through the pages of sensational artwork within this book. The diligence and creativity speaks for itself, and I can only hope you—as the viewer—enjoy the journey as much as we did creating it.

Charlie Wen
2011

WARRIOR OF TWO WORLDS

On film and in the comics, Marvel's heroes are known for one quality above all: They're human, relatable, with flaws just like yours and mine. Captain America was a scrawny young man who yearned to serve his country. Iron Man built his armor, piece by piece, with his own hands. Hawkeye and the Black Widow have no powers at all, just years of intensive combat training.

And then there's Thor.

"Thor is one of our more challenging characters," Executive Producer Craig Kyle says. "He's the least Marvel-ish of them—he's a god, he's an alien. So the way we tried to tackle that challenge was to translate that story in a way that would make Thor fans happy, but would also get people like my wife to enjoy the story."

Thor is a true hero—a warrior who will stand his ground in the face of all enemies, no matter how powerful or numerous. Yet he's still young by the standards of his people, and the burden of his heritage often weighs heavy on him. In crafting this sequel, Kyle says the studio began by looking at how the character had grown during the course of *Thor* and *Marvel's The Avengers*.

"Thor is not the petulant son that he was in the first film," Kyle says. "Not to say he's not still flawed. He absolutely is. He's just not that same man who was all heart and no mind. He's finding more center to his character."

Helming *Marvel's Thor: The Dark World* was a new director: Alan Taylor. "When I was first approached, I thought they had made a mistake and were calling the wrong guy," Taylor says, "because I was very much ensconced in television. I've never been a comic-book guy—I didn't grow up loving comics. But I loved the scale of *Thor*, and I had come to love epic language. That's something I got to experiment with in *Game of Thrones*, so that was enticing. The cast that had been assembled by Ken Branagh was a dream cast. I'd come to love having one foot in reality and one foot in fantasy, and all of those things came together here. Thor is a unique super hero because he carries so much weight of history and mythology."

Cover to *Thor: Tales of Asgard (1968) #1* by Jack Kirby with colors by Matt Milla.

Asgard, the Realm Eternal—as envisioned by writer Stan Lee and artist Jack Kirby in *Journey into Mystery Annual (1965) #1*, with colors by Matt Milla.

Kevin Feige, President of Marvel Studios, praises Taylor's visual approach. "Alan is bringing a grittier, more visceral, more textured patina to the designs of the worlds—and to Asgard, in particular. It's less to chase either *Game of Thrones* or *Lord of the Rings*, because you're not going to catch up. But part of the fun of Thor, over our other characters, is he doesn't have to stay on Earth."

In the first film, Thor traveled to Earth, an experience that grounded him in a familiar setting. This time, Earth scientist Jane Foster must undertake a perilous journey to the fabled land of Asgard.

"Now," Creative Executive Eric Carroll says, "the tables are turned so that Jane's the fish out of water in Thor's world."

"I think fans are going to be really excited to see her going to Asgard," Marvel Head of Visual Development Charlie Wen says, "because in the first movie, you never really got to see the two worlds coming together."

To Feige, the Thor/Jane Foster relationship "is the heart of the story. Really, they were only together for three days. Do they love each other? Do they like each other? Do they *know* each other? That love story in the first movie was essentially a quick crush, over the course of three days in the middle of the desert."

Framestore concept art

And our hero still has a lot of growing up to do. "Thor is incredibly relatable," Writer Chris Yost says. "He's a son, he's a brother; he's as human as you get. Over the course of *Thor*, he learned humility. And then in *Avengers*, he learned the true madness of his brother. He's in a much more responsible place now, but he's still got a lot to learn at the same time."

Crucial to that process—as always—is Thor's relationship with his adoptive brother, Loki. Once again, Loki appears by turns as Asgard's champion and its destroyer, his motives constantly shrouded in mystery.

"If you look at Loki," Kyle says, "we've seen him as the innocent man faced with the truth of his heritage. In the darkest ways, he tried to show that he is still the boy he believed himself to be in his father's eyes, and he failed. Then he acknowledged that he's a villain and decided he was just going to become what he's destined to be, and again he faltered. Now the question is, how do we get into that story and show a different side of him?"

"The first *Thor* movie was as much a Loki origin story as it was a Thor origin story," Feige says. "I really wanted the Marvel Cinematic Universe to have a villain as interesting as Magneto was, in the first *X-Men* film. Early on, we thought Loki had the best potential to do that."

But Loki is far from the only villain in this film. The larger threat comes from Malekith, leader of the Dark Elves. In choosing the villains, the filmmakers turned—as they often do—to the vast back catalogue of Thor comics.

Both Kyle and Carroll credit the strong influence of Walter Simonson, a popular writer/artist whose long run remains a high-water mark among fans. Simonson introduced both Malekith and the Dark Elves.

"When I was working on *Thor*, I researched myths and legends from all over Northern Europe," Simonson recalls. "I did a lot of reading on Celtic fairy stories of Great Britain, and I used some of the characteristics ascribed to the northern fairies for my Dark Elves—

Production still.

An awestruck Jane Foster accompanies Thor to the Realm Eternal, from *Thor (1966) #136* — written by Stan Lee, penciled by Jack Kirby and inked by Vince Colletta.

including their anathema to iron and mortal food. I gave Malekith his name, inspired by various names I came across in my reading. I used 'mal...' because of its association in French and Latin with 'bad,' 'ill,' 'wrong' and so on. And 'kith' means 'acquaintances' or 'neighbors.' The Dark Elves were closer in kind to humans than the gods and, in my stories, lived beneath the Earth, not so far from us."

Thor: The Dark World opens with a rousing battle in Vanaheim, an enlightened realm that's suddenly invaded by a band of alien marauders. "Vanaheim feels like a mixture of Irish browns and greens with the rich textures of coastal Italy," says Victoria Alonso—Executive Producer of *Thor: The Dark World*, and EVP of VFX and Post Production. "Then you have some signs that make you realize, 'Oh, we're not in Europe. We're elsewhere.' That's a combination of elements we try to include in all of our films—so it feels comfortable to be there, and yet it's not just around the corner."

While Thor engages his enemies in Vanaheim, Jane Foster and her intern, Darcy, discover a key to the invasion right here on Earth. That leads Jane to Asgard, the primary setting—and battleground—of the film.

Kyle welcomed the chance to show more of Asgard than was possible in the first film. "Although we defined the palace and the heart of Asgard, there's so much we haven't seen. Where are the bars, the stables, the commoners? Where's the age and the history? Where's the Asgard that Odin's grandfather built, and then his father after that, and then Odin? As we traverse Asgard in this film, you're going to see many more layers of history."

Concept Artist Jackson Sze agrees: "*Thor* established a spectacular realm of gleaming towers and fantastic architecture. Here, we wanted to give Asgard a more lived-in feel, with elements that are human-scale and filled with warmth."

Kyle credits the conception of Marvel's Asgard to Stan Lee and Jack Kirby, originators of the *Thor* comic. "Stan and Jack were very smart in the way they reengineered the Thor and Norse myths. It's not far from the Superman idea: If an alien fell to the planet, but instead of it happening in modern day it happened in ancient times, primitive man would see these characters as deities. They can fly, they can control the weather, they can survive nearly any attack or injury—so by all appearances, they are absolutely gods.

"So going in that direction, we engineered the Marvel cinematic history of our universe: Instead of the Norse creating the gods, it's the gods that created the Norse. Aliens came long ago, they were discovered by the early people of Norway, and the Norse were inspired by the incredible acts and feats and items of the Asgardians—so they shaped their culture in the gods' image."

The battle against Malekith leads Thor and his allies to their enemy's shadowy homeland: the devastated realm of Svartalfheim. "We moved from the lushness of Vanaheim to the cold, gray, raw, dead ice floes and rocks of Iceland for Svartalfheim—where nothing could exist, nothing could grow," Production Designer Charles Wood explains.

"Svartalfheim is a world in peril," Alonso adds. "It's empty of life—with rich dark ground and turbulent skies, and a thin light that is sort of painted out there."

"Part of the fun of Thor is that he doesn't have to stay on Earth," Feige says. "We think audiences are ready to go further with us into Asgard, into the other Nine Realms, into the mythology of Odin and Odin's family."

But Thor still bears a strong connection to Earth—because of Jane Foster, and because of his bond with the Avengers. "Thor is of two worlds," Carroll says. "He's got duties at home—but then he's also drawn to and very connected to Earth, as well. A big part of this film was him finding the right balance. Will he have to make a choice between the two realms, or will he find a way to be a man of both?"

Taylor agrees: "I imagine that Thor's story will be forever split between Asgard and the Nine Realms, and also Earth. Part of the challenge is to balance his godliness against the kind of humanity that we feel in him. So the story will always revolve tightly around Midgard, I think."

And it's not just *two* realms coming together. Faced with the challenge of topping the widescreen spectacle of *Marvel's The Avengers*, the filmmakers chose to focus on a smaller cast against a chaotic, ever-shifting battlefield. In *Thor: The Dark World*'s gripping, pyrotechnic climax, all Nine Realms threaten to crash together with devastating results.

"The laws of reality are going to be bent and broken," Kyle warns, "so the battlefield is unlike anything we've seen. Characters will begin fighting in one realm—Earth—then explode into another, and potentially back into our own. Buildings and other elements will be colliding. And our hero will have to navigate this while fighting the darkest forces he's ever faced."

Executive Producer Louis D'Esposito warns that character is always more important than visual effects. "Hopefully, the visual style is supporting the story all the

Malekith, from the cover to *Thor (1966) #345* by Walter Simonson with colors by Steve Oliff.

time, not standing out so you can separate them and say, `That looked good, but it wasn't such a good story.' We never want that. We want people to say, `I love that film, I love that story.'

"It's always the actors. Character first. It has to be."

"The *Thor* franchise has the benefit of an amazing cast," Carroll says. "Anthony Hopkins breathed life into Odin. And Natalie Portman, who plays Jane Foster. And Chris Hemsworth is Thor. And then there's Tom Hiddleston as Loki. He inhabits that character so well—it's just a lot of fun to watch."

Thor: The Dark World has a classic protagonist, a powerful script, a director with great credentials and a terrific cast—not to mention a strong set of roots.

"You look back and you realize that these guys, these visionaries—Stan Lee, Jack Kirby, Walter Simonson, the rest of them—they really did latch on to themes that are still relevant," Carroll says. "And even though times have changed, we try to pull the best stuff and put it together in an organic and interesting way—the theme of fathers and sons, and being brash but having to learn humility, and learning to use your power responsibly."

But moviemaking is never an exact science, Kyle cautions. "There's only so much you can plan for. Even if everything goes exactly as you plan, there's that extra ten percent that can never be accounted for or planned on. And it can elevate these films to places that the first *Iron Man* hit, that *Avengers* hit, that now *Iron Man 3* has hit—that creates extraordinary outcomes beyond anyone's wildest imagination."

At Marvel Studios, everyone's fingers are crossed.

Kyle sums up the process: "You start with the movie you *plan* to make. And then at the beginning of post-production, you discover the movie you *did* make. And by the time it's over, you hopefully have delivered the film you *wanted* to make—which is filled with surprises; some additional photography; lots of VFX; and a ton of blood, sweat and tears."

Knowing Thor, he wouldn't have it any other way.

Kurse, from the cover to *Thor (1966) #363* by Walter Simonson with colors by Steve Oliff.

CHAPTER ONE

RETURN TO THE GOLDEN REALM

In the first *Thor* film, the wars waged by Asgard spread to our world, threatening Earth's existence. This time around, the threat menaces *all nine* of the known worlds—beginning with the peaceful realm of Vanaheim.

"We wanted to come into the story and immediately acclimate people, get them caught up," Executive Producer Craig Kyle explains. "Vanaheim is a very peaceful planet, a race of scientists and philosophers, and they're not prepared for battle. But the place is overrun with marauders, and they're looting and robbing and doing horrible things. Suddenly, the Bifrost slams down in the middle of it all; the Warriors Three and Sif leap out like the four horsemen. And once the Bifrost clears, it reveals Thor."

"That's a big sequence," Fight Coordinator Ben Cooke says. "There's a lot going on; there are a lot of extras, a lot of background fights, a lot of battles—a lot of individual actor fights, as well."

"We get to see Vanaheim," Kyle adds, "which allows us to introduce our characters and show what they've been doing since their last adventures. The core nine worlds, or realms, are what we always focus on."

The siege of Vanaheim is a spectacular action sequence, the decisive battle in a year-long campaign waged by the Thunder God and his fellow warriors to restore order to the Nine Realms.

In any other film, this would be the dramatic climax. In *Marvel's Thor: The Dark World*, it's just the beginning.

Production still.

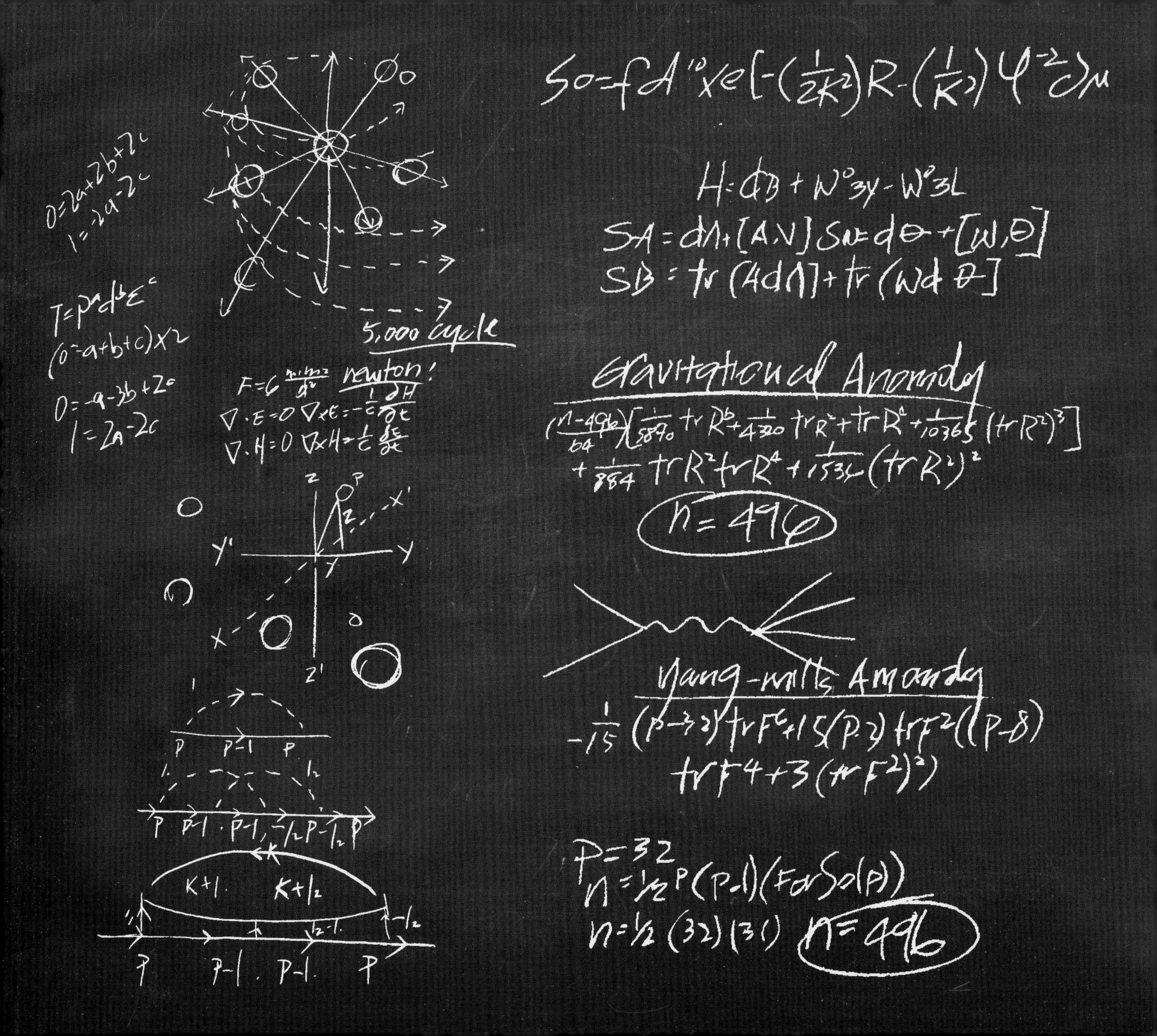

5,000 cycle

newton!

$\nabla \cdot E = 0$

$\nabla \cdot H = 0$

Gravitational Anomaly

$n = 496$

Yang-Mills Anomaly

$P = 32$

$n = \frac{1}{2}P(P-1)$

$n = \frac{1}{2}(32)(31)$

$n = 496$

The Book of Yggdrasil

The sacred Book of Yggdrasil was designed by Graphic Artist Jools Faiers, who describes it as "the Asgardians' equivalent of the Bible, kept in the depths of Odin's library. As Odin explains to Jane the origins of the Dark Elves, the illuminated pages depict the Elves' destruction as a direct result of Asgard's creation."

Corner braces: Those Who Sit Above in Shadow

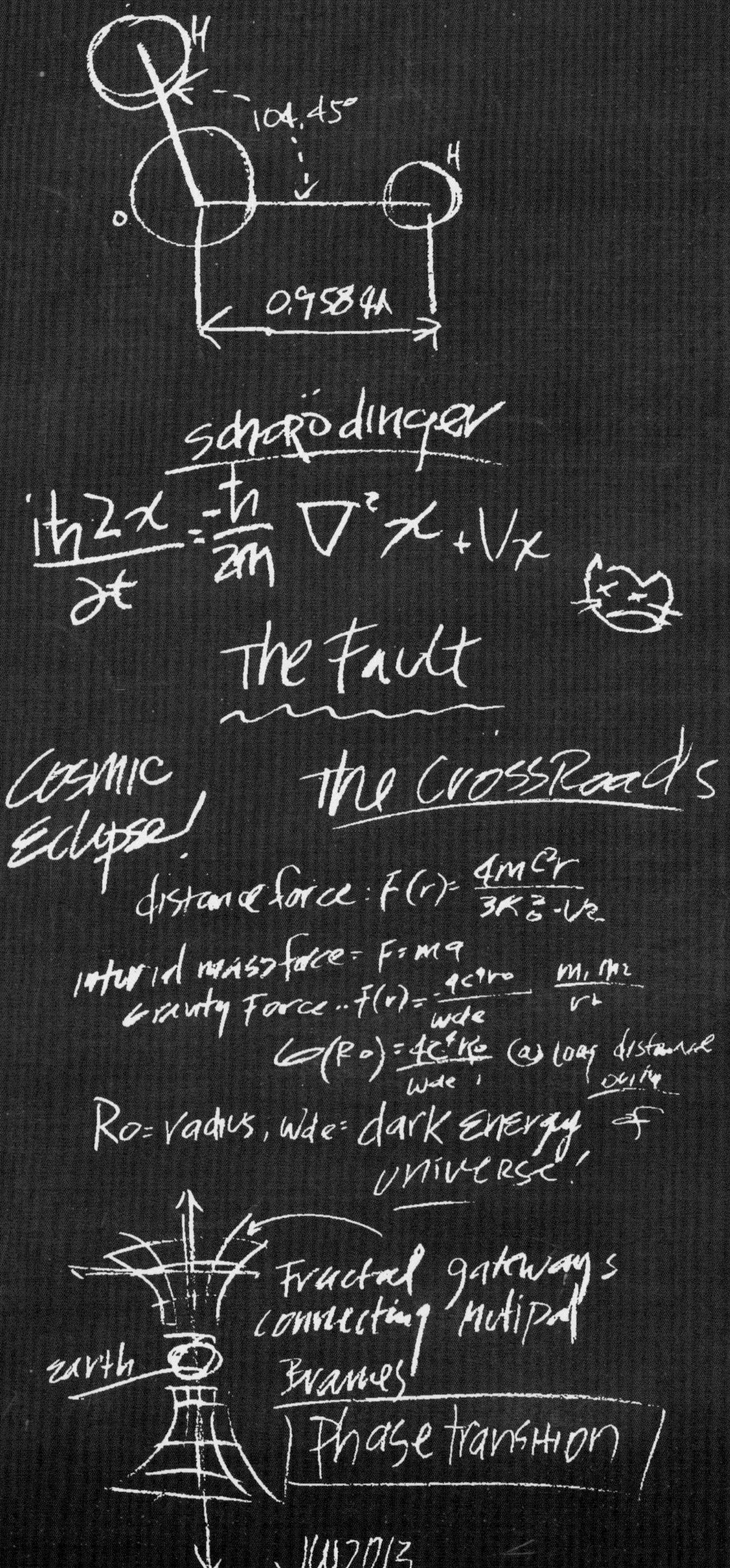

From the research files of Dr. Jane Foster and Dr. Erik Selvig:
The science behind the impending Convergence that may destroy the Earth

Notes for the layman:

- **Gravitational anomaly:** any major disruption of gravity—in this case, a black hole
- **Yang-Mills anomaly:** a disruption of the basic principles of particle physics, particularly as applied to the Weak and Electromagnetic Forces
- **616 Universe:** designation applied by the Omniversal Majestrix of Otherworld to distinguish the Marvel Universe from an infinite number of parallel worlds, first used in *The Daredevils #7 (1983)*
- **Nine Realms:** the ancient Norse conception of the universe, first depicted in *Journey Into Mystery #85 (1962)*
- **Simonson's Theory of Relativity:** apparently a physics concept attributed to Writer/Artist/Quantum Hobbyist Walter Simonson—see *Thor #337 (1983)* and later
- **Nexus of All Reality:** location in the Florida Everglades where parallel worlds sometimes intersect—first seen in *Fear #13 (1973)*
- **The Alignment:** the moment, once every five thousand years, when the Realms align and the Convergence becomes possible
- **Schrodinger:** Austrian physicist—a pioneer in the fields of quantum theory, wave mechanics, and feline irradiation
- **The Fault:** a rip in the fabric of the universe, first seen in *War of Kings #6 (2009)*
- **Cosmic Eclipse:** the point at which the black hole of Svartalfheim intersects with all Nine Realms
- **The Crossroads:** gateway dimension consisting primarily of portals to other worlds—see *Incredible Hulk #300 (1984)* and later
- **Brane:** mathematical concept used in string theory
- **Phase Transition:** the transformation of one state of matter to another
- **Dark Energy of the Universe:** long-theorized source of Malekith's power, manifested through the black hole of Svartalfheim

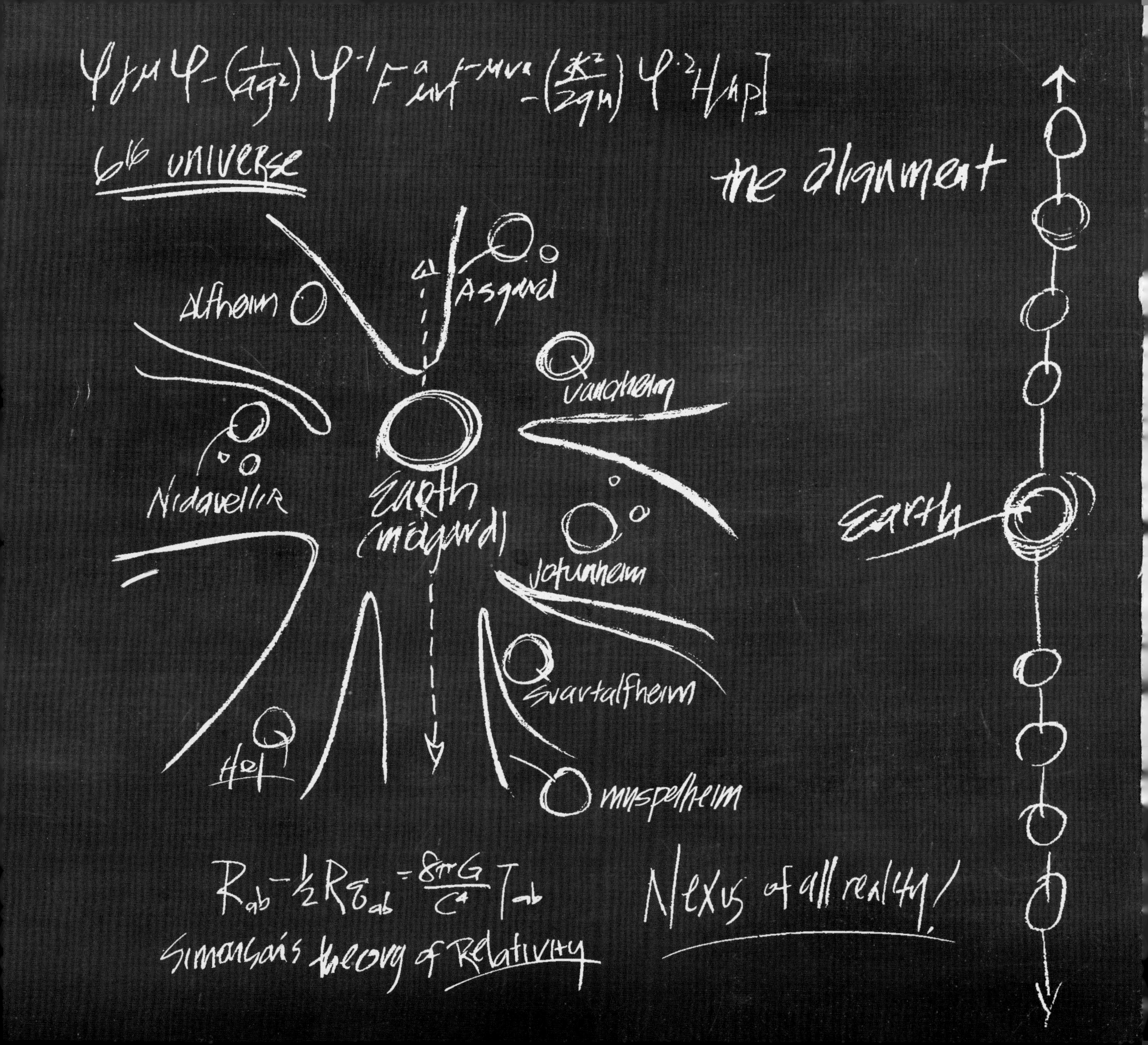

$\psi J\mu\psi - \left(\frac{1}{4g^2}\right)\psi^{-1} F^{a}_{\mu\nu} F^{\mu\nu a} - \left(\frac{k^2}{2g\mu}\right)\psi^{-2} H_{\mu\rho}]$

616 UNIVERSE

the alignment

Alfheim

Asgard

Vanaheim

Nidavellir

Earth
(midgard)

Jotunheim

Svartalfheim

Hel

muspelheim

Earth

$$R_{ab} - \frac{1}{2} R g_{ab} = \frac{8\pi G}{c^4} T_{ab}$$

Simonson's theory of Relativity

Nexus of all reality!

"The book had to look like a treasured relic—so the paper, cover tooling, and metal clasp and plates all needed to be reminiscent of a real illuminated book. I scanned a wealth of source materials—including the Book of Kells, the Lindisfarne gospels and Russian iconography—to collect design elements that I felt suitable."

The birth of light shattered the darkness bringing death to the Dark Elves

The elves fought the light that radiated from Asgard. They built a weapon out of the darkness and unleashed the dark power of the Aether across the Nine Realms inflicting the torment of war.

"The paper used in the book is man-made, but has an aged look and a weight that gives a great crunchy crackle sound as it turns. The colors had to look subtle, faded by aging, yet bright enough to have the visual impact of pouring out the light of Asgard. So there is a considerable amount of gold leaf on every page—especially the creation page, where the gold glow shows on the actors' faces."

Svartalfheim: The genesis of Aether

Aurora: Brings the end of darkness.

THE BIRTH OF THE NINE REALMS

From out of the cold darkness of the universe came forth the first dawn of light. Born of a spark of golden energy the ethereal light filled the far reaches of the universe. The majesty of the immaculate Aurora heralded the creation of the Nine Realms and banished all...

(banished all...) the dark creatures to the voids of obscurity as the golden warmth nurtured the sparks of light. Thus the Nine Realms were born and within the core of this new universe came forth the Yggdrasil and each realm found its natural position within the branches from the tree of life. From this time forth Yggdrasil and the realms will always be bathed in the glorious light radiating from the mighty Asgard and from the gods.

THOR

The makers of a sequel always face a tricky balancing act: maintaining the elements that audiences related to in the first film, while simultaneously deepening and broadening the cinematic experience. For Marvel Head of Visual Development Charlie Wen, those challenges came together squarely in the character of Thor himself.

"When we started on the first *Thor* film, it was about defining an entirely new world in the Marvel Cinematic Universe. For the heroes, like Thor, we started with design elements drawn from the Jack Kirby era of Thor comics with the accompanying inspiration of classic Norse mythology. The Norse elements were evident, but minimized and abstracted due to the Kirby influence and the idea of turning Thor into a modern-day super hero, not just a warrior.

"There was a sense of theatricality in the comics, especially with Thor. He was larger than life, with high shoulders and a cape that was constantly billowing. There was an absolute level of simplicity, no superficial textures or reliefs on the armor; it was more about focusing on interesting shapes and materials that we had never seen before. With that being said, I still wanted all of the heroes to have enough connection to Earth to feel real, but alien enough to feel different than a typical warrior.

"When we began development on *Thor: The Dark World*, Alan Taylor, Craig Kyle and Kevin Feige wanted to turn Asgard into a place that was a bit more humanized. The redesigns of the characters, like Thor, began with creating textures—utilizing materials like leather, gold and iron that were closer to Earth-based materials.

"But even more than that, it was about taking the theatrical elements of the first *Thor* film and peeling away the mystery and idealization, while introducing the understandable and practical. At first look, the audience should be able to understand how the materials of the suit meld together and how the mechanisms, like fasteners and belts, work.

"When the audience sees Thor's new look, it is easy to identify how the leather and Norse-based knotting work together to create the functioning elements of a warrior, while still retaining elements of his regal heritage."

Thor—the man—is also a work in progress. "Tony Stark wasn't perfect at the end of the first *Iron Man*, and I don't think Thor was perfect at the end of *Thor*—particularly in his relationship with his brother," says Kevin Feige, President of Marvel Studios. "There's also a question of what happens when you're now ready for something, but don't necessarily want it anymore. That's part of his internal struggle."

Charlie Wen concept art.

Charlie Wen concept art.

"Chris Hemsworth was born to play this role," Director Alan Taylor says. "People say that about many characters and many actors, but I've never been so aware of it being true. Chris, besides being sort of physically perfect, has a voice that carries such weight. You actually can believe that this young man has a stature that's more than human. He's not just a pretty face."

Production still.

Charlie wen keyframe.

MJOLNIR

Thor's fabled hammer underwent a redesign, as well. "As with Thor himself, I wanted to weave a little more Norse knot work into the design—namely, in the handle area," Charlie Wen says. "We also implemented, subtly, the rough shape of the Norse symbol for Mjolnir at the base, near the leather holding strap."

The evolution of Mjolnir — as featured in *Thor*, *Marvel's The Avengers* and *Thor: The Dark World*.

Pattern detail

Rune inscription:
"Whosoever holds this hammer if he be worthy shall possess the power of Thor."

Jools Faiers concept art.

VOLSTAGG

Volstagg, Hogun and Fandral—Asgard's Warriors Three—all received subtle makeovers. According to Charlie Wen, those changes worked in tandem with the overall plan for the film.

"The redesign of Volstagg, like the other Warriors, was more about conveying a sense of understanding of how the suit works, how the pieces work together, what the practical elements of the suit are—not simply giving him a new costume.

"We also see a glimpse of Volstagg's family life in *Thor: The Dark World*. So with his costume, we were also given the opportunity to integrate his home life into the design. This gave us a chance to construct pieces and utilize fabrics that related to his life outside the battlefield—and how, in turn, he would use these pieces on the battlefield."

"The overall mandate for this sequel was to design everything in a more realistic and relatable way," Concept Artist Andy Park says. "The armor should be more lived-in, less pristine and clean. So everything went in that direction, down to the hairstyles.

"I was able to update Volstagg's look to reflect this. You can really believe that he has seen thousands of battles and is not someone you want to upset."

"Volstagg is this giant character, just such a devourer of life," Craig Kyle says. "He eats everything, he drinks everything, he loves greatly, he has the most children—actually, he's the only one with children. So he's just this character of deep heart and emotion. I think he fights passionately because he loves so deeply the people that he leaves behind when he goes to battle, and all the innocents of the world."

Andy Park concept art.

Production still.

HOGUN

"Hogun's costume required minimal tweaking, as Marvel was happy with the way he looked in *Thor*," Concept Artist Jackson Sze says. "We added fabric and texture details to provide visual interest in the costume. Hogun is a Vanir in this universe, so I placed him on the mountain peaks of his homeland, ready to defend his people."

Charlie Wen adds, "With Hogun, we stripped away some of the strictly 'samurai' look from the first film and implemented elements of the Vanir: tribal influences, as well as Mongol and other Asian influences. This allowed us to break down the design motifs into smaller details that work in tandem with elements that Charlie Wood crafted for the world of the Vanirs, including their technology and architecture."

"The Warriors Three are an important part of Thor's storyline," Craig Kyle says. "They're his dear friends; they grew up with him. He's always been prince; he's always been heir to the throne. But it's the people who are with you when you're young who can always tell you when you're being a jerk, or when you're being less than you should be. They keep you honest as you get older."

"I find the Warriors Three very challenging because they come from three completely different cultures," Alan Taylor says. "From the looks of it, they're Robin Hood and Genghis Khan and Falstaff. I was looking at some of the comics and loved their banter, their dialogue. We're letting them be warriors more this time, not just comic relief. Trying to serve them as real, distinct characters—each of whom has a different relationship to Thor, so they don't just come out of a generic chorus. We're grounding them more in a sense of lived reality."

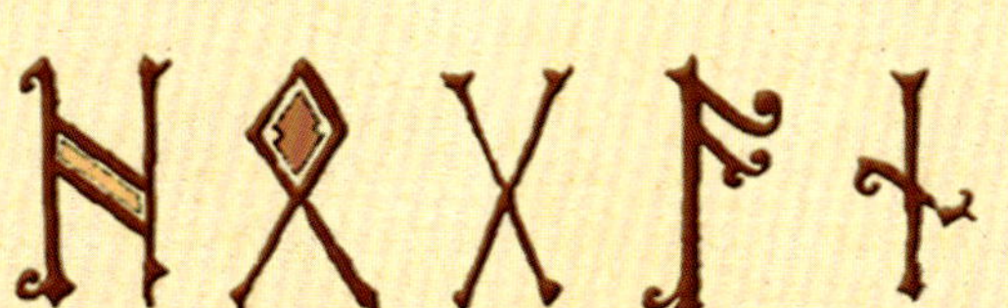

Jackson Sze concept art.

Production still.

FANDRAL

"Fandral was a fun one to design," Jackson Sze recalls. "We kept the spirit of his original costume and adjusted his proportions for the new actor, Zachary Levi. Fandral's flamboyant character lent itself to a showy costume: cape, jewelry, etc.

"The design was a collaborative effort between Justin Sweet, Andrew Kim and me. Zachary Levi was keen to be blond in the movie, so we tried different hairstyles. I wanted to channel his character through his stance and surroundings. He is confident and proud."

Charlie Wen agrees: "The design is reminiscent of Fandral's look from the first *Thor* film. Our only challenge was tailoring it to a taller actor."

Property Master Barry Gibbs recalls one alternation particular to Fandral, however. "We changed his weapon from a saber to more of an épée because they wanted him to do more of a thrusting style of fighting, as opposed to slashing."

Craig Kyle discusses the change of actors: "Zach was someone we talked to early on—he was doing the series *Chuck* and really busy, but we had some great discussions. Then we had a situation where we lost our Fandral, and the actor we'd *first* talked to, originally, became available. So we were very fortunate that we had two talented actors tasked with the same role, and they each brought their own unique sense of humor and charisma to the character. Zach just came in and made Fandral his own from the very first scene."

Jackson Sze concept art.

Production still.

SIF

As the primary female warrior in the Thor saga, Sif holds a special place in the chronicles of Asgard.

"We wanted to take what was successful with Sif's design in the first film—the idea that she is a warrior and can take on a challenge just as well, if not better, than her male warrior counterparts—and take it to the next level," Charlie Wen says, "while also creating, as with the other warriors, a sense of understanding of how the armor functions on a practical level.

"Sif has a larger range of motion with her updated look, due to the addition of breakups within the solid pieces of her armor. That greatly facilitated her ability to move freely while wielding a sword, riding a horse or even just standing and breathing."

Craig Kyle sees Sif as Thor's conscience, in a way. "No one wants to be the nag in the group, but girls have the strength and the courage to just say whatever needs to be said—especially when the boys who have a lot of potential aren't using it. So she tends to be that voice."

"Jaimie Alexander is perfect to portray the Lady Sif," Andy Park adds. "She has both the beauty and ferocity needed to be a loyal ally and friend to Thor, as well as a worthy combatant to fight alongside him."

Andy Park concept art.

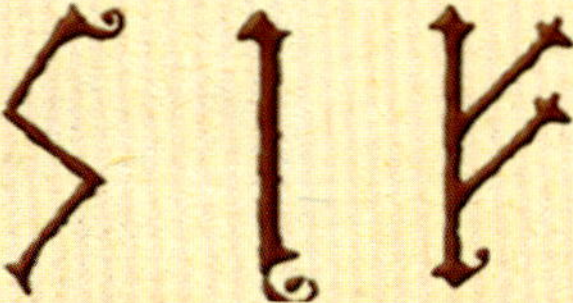

Production still.

Framestore/J.McCoy concept art.

The filmmakers faced the challenge of bringing several new realms to life. Vanaheim, the first one we see, is a tranquil, idyllic setting—until the marauders attack.

"Originally, we looked at a lot of locations in China and in Bolivia," Production Designer Charles Wood explains. "We wanted to find something that was forested, and something that had strange and unusual rock formations.

"Early on, it looked as though the people were going to have more of a tribal culture—but we didn't want to do something that was stereotypical. So we ended up looking at a lot of different early architectural types: Mayan, early Christian, Asian, and different religious orders and influences. We took influence from many different types of architecture, little bits and pieces of them, and then amalgamated them into something that could become Vanaheim. We basically wanted to see something that was nomadic, and something that was ancient.

"The problem is, if you default to something like Mayan, it's been done before—it's very Indiana Jones. If you default to something else, that's probably been done before, too. So we tried to mix many things together."

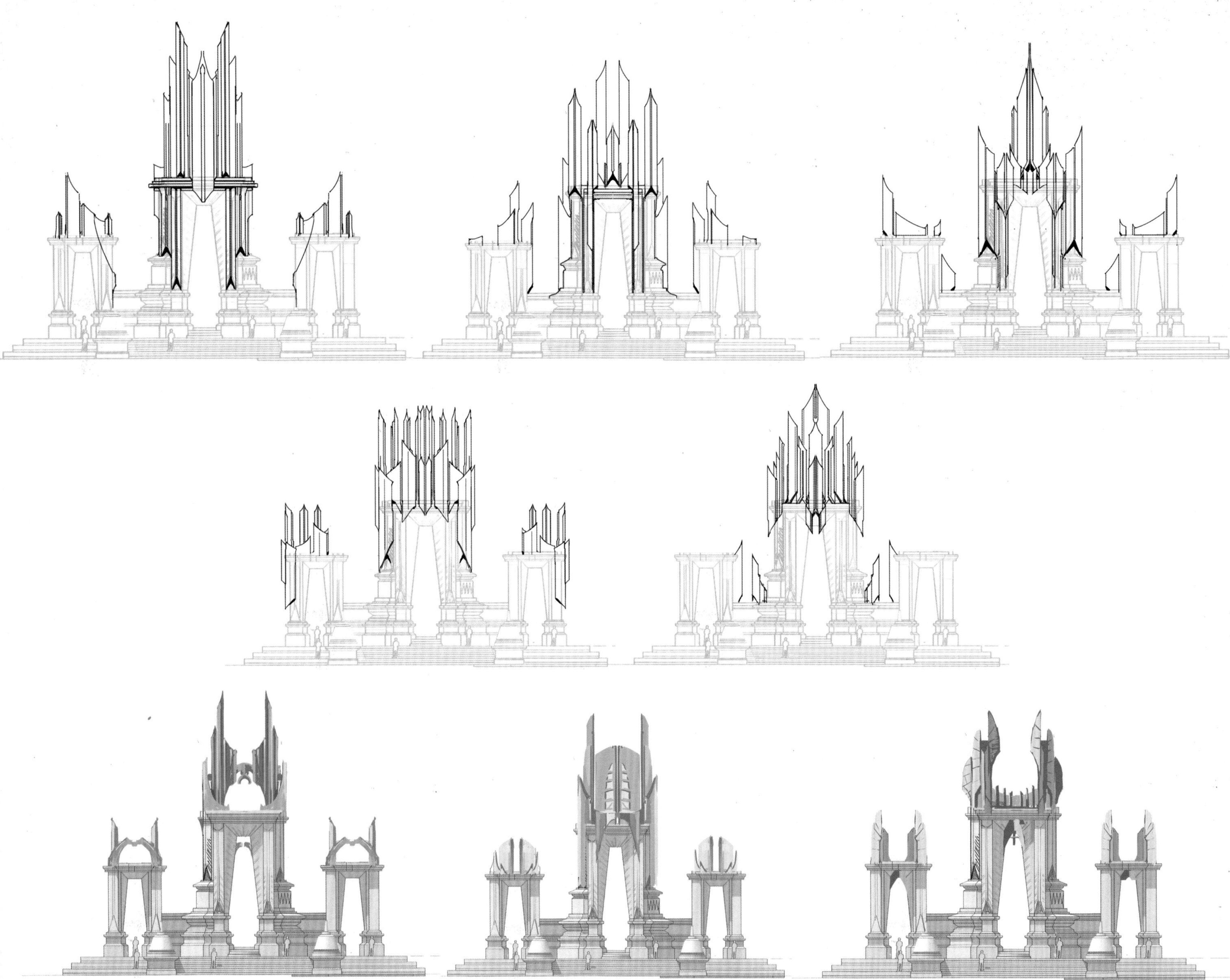

Framestore concept art.

"Vanaheim was shot traditionally in Bourne Wood, in the Southeast of the United Kingdom," Visual Effects Supervisor Jake Morrison reveals. "This location offers beautiful imagery. It also offered great access—something we needed for a shoot with over 200 extras and stunts players in full costume and, in some cases, very elaborate prosthetics. We knew we would have to alter Bourne Wood to make it less Earth-like, so we planned for set extensions. While much of the original Bourne Wood exists in the picture, the background environment has been massively extended to give an otherworldly feel. Vanaheim's signature double-ring monoliths are straight from the mind of Charlie Wood."

Wood: "Because we wanted the culture to seem tribal and we wanted to ground these people into the environment they're living within, yurts [portable dwellings] seemed an obvious way to go. But rather than having all the structure on the inside of the yurt, we built a lot of them out of bronze. We tried to make them feel more permanent."

Framestore/Kevin Jenkins concept art.

As in all Marvel films, the balance between physical locations and visual effects was crucial to achieving the look of Vanaheim—and the other realms, as well.

Morrison: "More from an aesthetic point of view than because of a production constraint, we tried to be sparing with the set extensions. We wanted to avoid distracting the audience from the action and emotional content. That meant we mainly concentrated the efforts on wider battle shots. Wherever you would get production value for an extension, we added a little—sometimes no more than a distant, alien-looking silhouette to give the scene an otherworldly feel."

Wood adds, "It's a process of mixing things we are familiar with as an audience and adding magical strangeness to them. The yin and the yang of it.

"Then, within the environments themselves, Visual Effects would take these strange, mountainous forms and graft on a jungle, and extend them into geological forms that are not impossible, but verging on it. So everything we try to do involves taking an idea that is more rooted, and then growing it into something that is odd, even slightly disturbing."

Victoria Alonso—Executive Producer, and EVP of VFX and Post Production—agrees: "The locations give us something, but not everything. We take anything we can that is real, and then create the rest of it digitally. But at least the environment—the light, all of that—is something that the human eye recognizes and doesn't doubt."

Framestore/Kevin Jenkins concept art.

THE VANIR

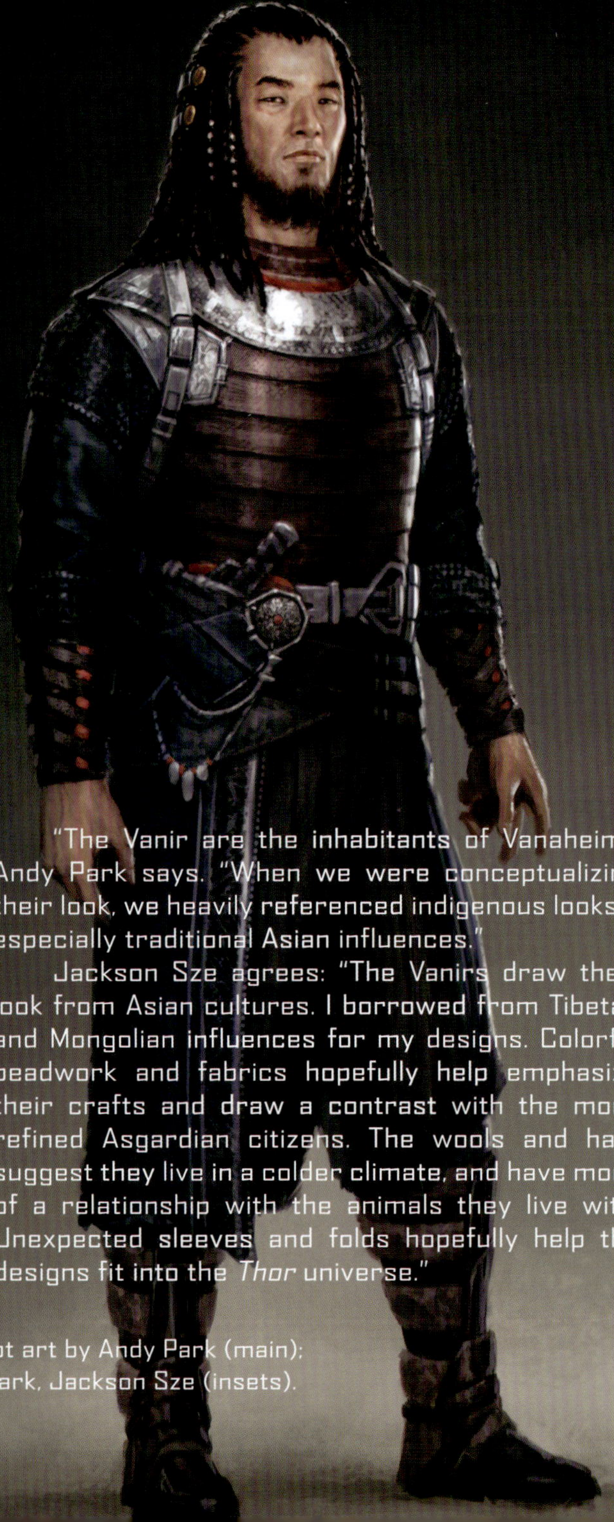

"The Vanir are the inhabitants of Vanaheim," Andy Park says. "When we were conceptualizing their look, we heavily referenced indigenous looks—especially traditional Asian influences."

Jackson Sze agrees: "The Vanirs draw their look from Asian cultures. I borrowed from Tibetan and Mongolian influences for my designs. Colorful beadwork and fabrics hopefully help emphasize their crafts and draw a contrast with the more refined Asgardian citizens. The wools and hats suggest they live in a colder climate, and have more of a relationship with the animals they live with. Unexpected sleeves and folds hopefully help the designs fit into the *Thor* universe."

Concept art by Andy Park (main);
Andy Park, Jackson Sze (insets).

THE MARAUDERS

In the film's first major battle, Thor and the warriors of Asgard face off against armored, helmeted marauders. Concept Artist Justin Sweet credits Charlie Wen with allowing illustrators leeway during the initial design stages.

"The marauders were very open as far as design," Sweet says. "The direction from Charlie was just, 'Do some cool marauders. We need some of these space-pirate guys—do whatever you feel like doing.' I did my first few, and they immediately got a good response."

Jackson Sze adds, "As far as the marauders go, the aesthetic was 'kit-bash grungy space pirates.' So they are oily, dirty, rough and well-worn—with armor that has been battle-proven and, in the best-case scenario, can come across as smelly.

"For the two marauders rogues' gallery spreads, I basically went through the different types of aliens that have appeared in the Thor comics and tried to find a good variety to include. We ended up with a Kronan, some Chitauri, Frost Giants and a few original designs—including some from Jacob Johnston, our department's coordinator.

"We were exploring alternative costumes and possible species. The more variety, the better."

Jackson Sze concept art.

"The marauders are made up of many races that have come together like pirates," Concept Artist Josh Nizzi says. "Their clothing and weapons are a mishmash of stolen and bartered gear from around the galaxy. When you face a marauder, you can never be sure what you might be up against."

"My first inspiration was the early *Star Wars* movies," Sweet adds. "Peeling paint on ships and Boba Fett. I went from there, and thought of cool shapes and colors and things to put on the Marauders. I just roughed them out, and they evolved from there."

Concept art by Justin Sweet (main); Jackson Sze (top insets); Jackson Sze, Justin Sweet (bottom insets).

Concept art by Justin Sweet (main, bottom insets); Josh Nizzi (top insets).

Jackson Sze concept art.

Justin Sweet concept art.

"The helmets were a mixed bag of original designs and modifications to existing props," Sze notes. "Mostly, I tried to work on variations of a theme. One theme was 'metal patchwork' and another was 'stitched leather.'

"Since they need to make a lot of these for the extras, we tried to keep it cost-effective by modifying existing props. We added elements like bones, teeth and goggles to add history and character."

Justin Sweet concept art with behind-the-scenes stills (insets).

Marauders prosthetics.

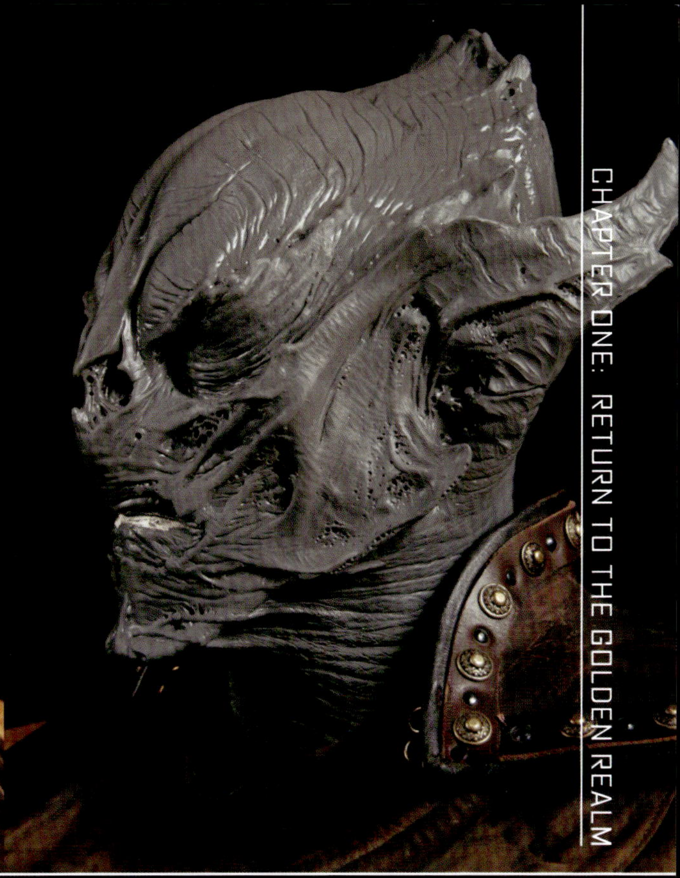

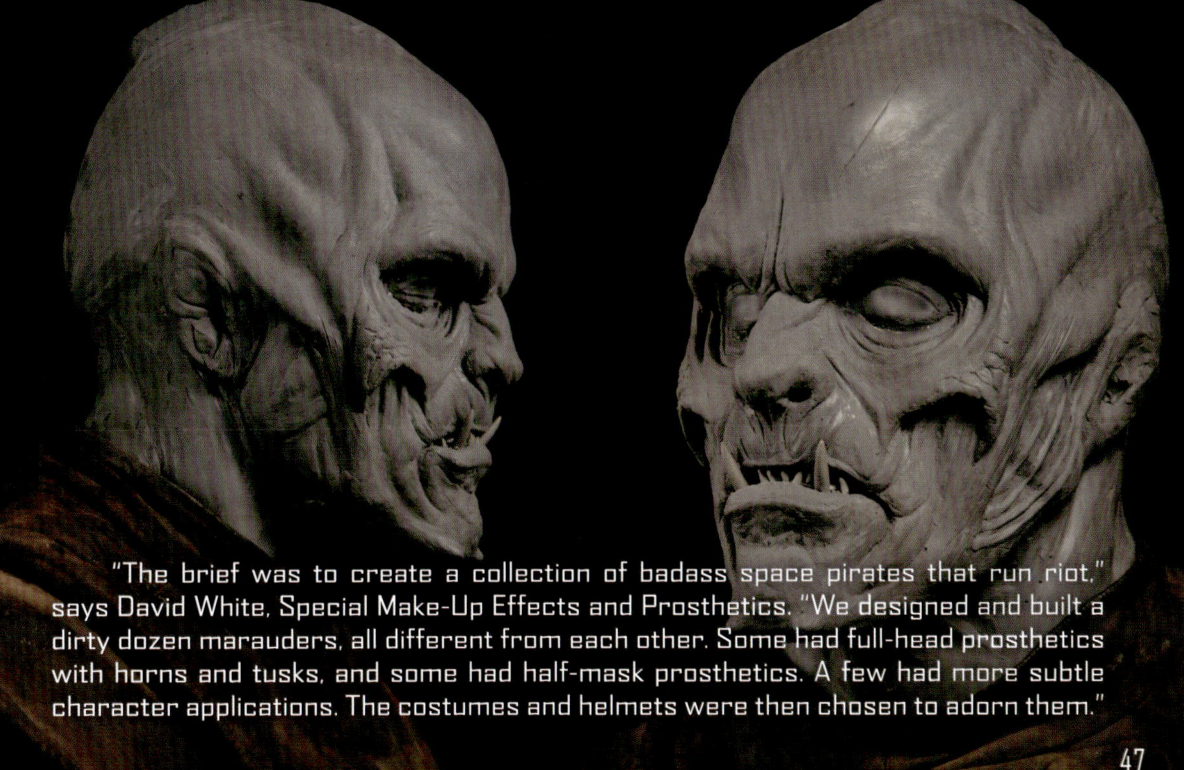

"The brief was to create a collection of badass space pirates that run riot," says David White, Special Make-Up Effects and Prosthetics. "We designed and built a dirty dozen marauders, all different from each other. Some had full-head prosthetics with horns and tusks, and some had half-mask prosthetics. A few had more subtle character applications. The costumes and helmets were then chosen to adorn them."

Marauders prosthetics.

"Keeping the prosthetics looking organic required my super-talented crew to use the most lifelike materials and techniques," White says. "I try to design everything nice and thin so the actor's face isn't buried under prosthetics and they can deliver their performance knowing that every facial gesture is recognized. You could theoretically walk to the store, if you could make it past Marvel security!"

Charlie Wen keyframe.

KRONAN STONE-MAN

Thor's brief battle against the Kronan Stone-Man drew cheers from audiences when it was shown in the theatrical trailer.

"Kronan makes his cinematic debut as he confronts Thor in the midst of the marauders' attack on the Vanir people," Andy Park says. "Unfortunately, it's a short-lived cameo, as he is instantly obliterated by the mighty Mjolnir."

Thor battled "the Stone Men from Saturn" in his very first appearance: 1962's *Journey Into Mystery #83*. That early encounter inspired this sequence in *Thor: The Dark World*.

Andy Park concept art.

"We made a Stone-Man, sculpted by Andrew Hunt and Martin Rezard," David White says. "It was then molded and made in fiberglass, then painted up and used on set as a VFX aid to establish the look and color in natural-situ lighting. This was the basis for the final VFX creation."

Stone-Man VFX aid.

KRONAN/THOR BATTLE

STORYBOARDS BY STEVE MARKOWSKI WITH RICK NEWSOME

"The Stone-Man fight was originally conceived to solve a story problem with Thor's Vanaheim battle: The sequence had no real climax," Storyboard Artist Steve Markowski explains. "The marauders seemed to me to surrender too abruptly. I thought that for them to suddenly throw down their arms and give up, Thor had to do something big. If Thor made short work of their biggest, toughest warrior, I thought that might motivate the surrender. Plus, it gave us the opportunity to place a very prominent tribute to Thor's first appearance—to see him battle the very first nemesis he encountered in the comics. The comic fan in me loved that. It was also a great opportunity for humor."

"I also think that in the early sequences of a super-hero movie, it's a good idea to make the hero look as impressive as possible," Markowski continues. "It's fun to see them defeat 'normal' bad guys with ease and see just how cool they are before you roll out the main villain. The main villain has to be a serious threat—as powerful or more powerful than the hero. In fact, he often defeats the hero at some point. So your opportunity to make the hero shine comes earlier on, when he can take out some minor criminals in impressive and entertaining ways."

Storyboard Artist Rick Newsome produced final revisions to Markowski's storyboards. "The Stone-Man gag is a nod to the first appearance of Thor in Marvel Comics' *Journey into Mystery #83*, where he faces 'the Stone Men from Saturn,'" Newsome says. "My contribution on these pages was basically the prolongation of Steve's setup. The gag itself was all his idea, from scratch."

Andy Park keyframe with VFX still (inset).

Markowski says the Stone-Man sequence came directly out of the open environment fostered by Craig Kyle, in which the artists were encouraged to suggest ideas and gags. "Like me, Craig comes from an animation background, and feels that some great contributions can come from the artists working on the film. When the storyboard artists were all finally able to get together with him in one room, he not only thanked me for my notes, but also encouraged everyone to do likewise and send him their thoughts. Had Craig not been so open and encouraging of us to send our suggestions, I probably never would have sent him my suggestion for the Kronan scene.

"It was really a great environment. One of the nice things about Marvel is that the people making these movies are more than just employees—they're also fans. I think that's why everyone at the studio was attracted to the Stone-Man idea. They're fans—they love the original material, and they love adapting it to the movie screen. And I think this shows in the films."

Production still.

CHAPTER TWO
BORN OF ETERNAL NIGHT

Every hero needs his enemies, and Thor finds more than his share in *Marvel's Thor: The Dark World*. From the realm of Svartalfheim come Kurse and the Dark Elves, led by the evil Malekith.

Victoria Alonso—Executive Producer, and EVP of VFX and Post Production—explains, "Malekith is in search of the Aether, which is what this movie really is about. Whoever has the Aether has the power—but humans shouldn't have it, because it can kill them. And that's Jane's journey. But Malekith is a really, really bad guy, and he doesn't have any regard for humanity or life."

Like many of the film's characters, these villains have their roots in the Thor comic books.

"Malekith and the Dark Elves were just intriguing characters," Creative Executive Eric Carroll says. "What we did was pull them out of the comics, dust them off, give them a cinematic makeover and so on. What we landed on was something we thought made sense with the story, and had a cool and creepy look."

And Malekith's homeworld is as fearsome as the villain himself: charred, barren, lifeless. "Svartalfheim is the realm of the Dark Elves," Carroll says. "So the title *The Dark World* is based on the idea that the threat comes from the realm of Svartalfheim."

Atomhawk Design concept art.

THE ARK

One of the first big visuals seen in the film is the Dark Elves' huge, menacing Ark.

"The Ark is this massive mother ship carrying the last of the Dark Elves," Executive Producer Craig Kyle explains. "In the prologue of the film, you can actually see a whole armada of ships in a scene set back when they had many thousands of them. The soldiers, the Dark Elf women and children, families—the entirety of their kind—lived in those ships. And Malekith forces all those ships to the ground, eliminating 90 percent of his species in a desperate attempt to have one more shot at the future."

According to Production Designer Charles Wood, the challenge with the Ark was "trying to come up with a design that was unique. There's been a lot of great spaceships created in the last twenty, thirty, forty years of filmmaking. It's quite a trick to come up with something that hasn't been seen before. So there were many, many, many concepts done of different types of vehicles before we got to the final design."

Atomhawk Design concept art.

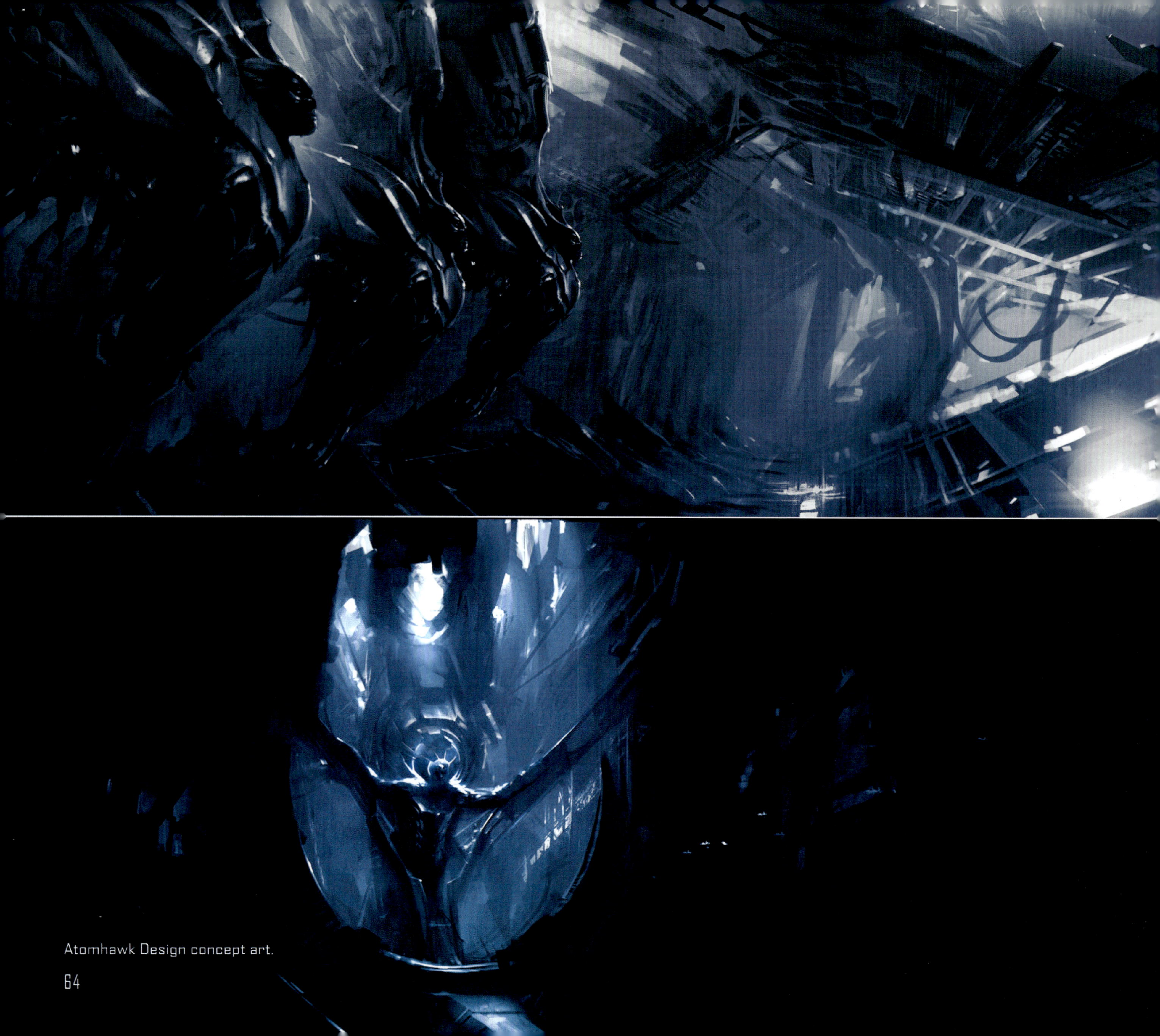

Atomhawk Design concept art.

Cumron Ashtiani, Art Director of Atomhawk Design, emphasizes the importance of "getting away from the mainstream spacecraft designs normally seen in the sci-fi world. We covered a lot of ground quickly in order to exhaust all the preconceptions and generic influences that the artists might have lurking in their minds. Once all the expected designs have been purged, then the really interesting ideas started to come out.

"We were given references of rock formations, charred organic matter, bird wings and gothic architecture to work from. The mother ship almost looks like a giant, rock-hewn cathedral in space. The idea is that this is not only Malekith's flagship, but also an ark for the Dark Elves to leave their home world indefinitely.

"The development of the mother ship was interesting in that it was a big collaborative effort, and the design was both refined in concept art and by the clay-modeling team at the studio. The ship was explored in both 2D and 3D simultaneously, and we created more than 80 pieces of the concept art in its development."

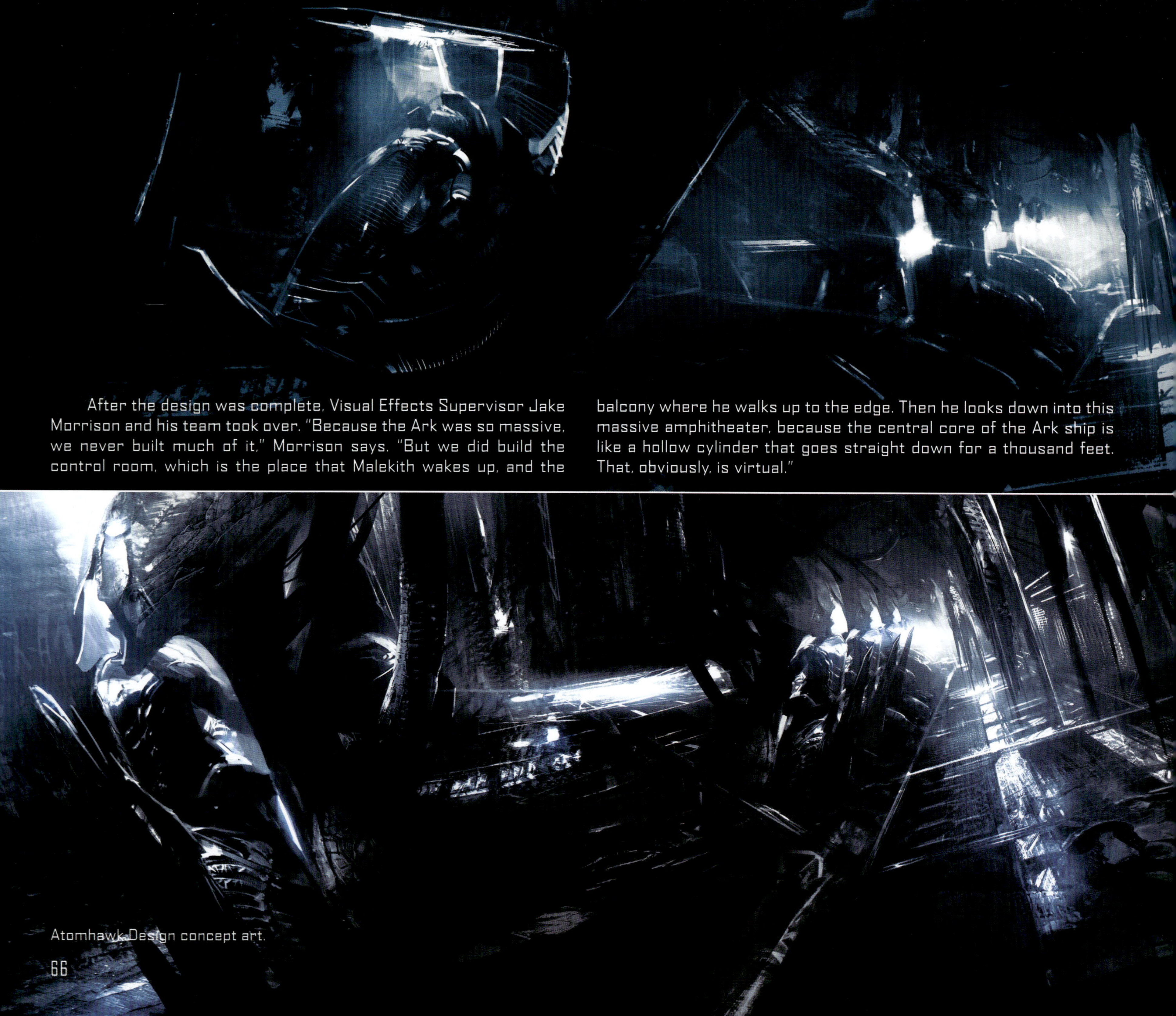

After the design was complete, Visual Effects Supervisor Jake Morrison and his team took over. "Because the Ark was so massive, we never built much of it," Morrison says. "But we did build the control room, which is the place that Malekith wakes up, and the balcony where he walks up to the edge. Then he looks down into this massive amphitheater, because the central core of the Ark ship is like a hollow cylinder that goes straight down for a thousand feet. That, obviously, is virtual."

Atomhawk Design concept art.

"We had one piece of initial concept art that we worked from, and then Double Negative—our lead Visual Effects house on this film—just filled in the details to an amazing degree," Morrison continues. "They built in an astounding level of finish to the whole thing, which you probably don't see enough in the picture for the amount of love and care that we lavished on it. But it is most certainly there."

The textures—the materials the Dark Elves had used to construct their fictional Ark—were as important to Wood as its physical shape. "We tried to find a material that was unrecognizable and that was also lifeless. We couldn't use metal; we couldn't use typical materials that could be part of a flying machine. We were really looking at charcoal—basically an inanimate object that's being burnt, and all of the water and life has come out in a blackened form.

"From that point, we studied burnt wood; we studied slate formations; and we amalgamated dark, oily slate and slate-puddle forms and carbonized surfaces. In the end, we came up with these strange, abstract, somewhat horrifying machines."

Within the Ark, the last surviving Dark Elves stand immobile, linked to the ship itself.

"It's kind of a stasis thing," Morrison explains. "They're in there, and Malekith—their leader—has been in stasis for quite a while. And then they wake up. Those are kind of pods they're in—the design on those is straight from the tortured-genius mind of Charlie Wood. He makes some pretty amazing stuff."

Paul Catling concept art.

The Ark went through several rounds of designs. "The final version is more militarized," Morrison says. "The initial concepts were beautiful and quite cadaver-ish—the silhouette was a kind of hanging almost-cruciform with what everyone calls witchy-fingers, with frayed, ragged ends. There was this beautiful early concept art of a 'golden sunset' moment, with clouds everywhere. And the mother ship is descending from the sky over Odin's palace, dwarfing it in scale. It was an aggressive pose, but all you really saw was this beautiful silhouette with these witchy-fingers and torn tentacle pieces—almost like a spinal column."

Production stills.

"It was a beautiful design," Morrison continues. "The trouble was that when the Ark was an aggressor—when it actually had to come in contact with something—some of those loose pieces looked as though they'd snap off. So we ended up making it a little more recognizably like a battleship, giving it an all-around tech upgrade. The final look is a lot beefier and a lot stronger, and should resonate with people as being an alien craft a lot quicker."

MALEKITH

In crafting Malekith, the film's primary villain, the artists faced a series of unique challenges.

"Malekith's portrayal in the Marvel comic books has a very extreme look—somewhere between a medieval court jester and an '80s glam-rock star," Concept Artist Andy Park explains. "So translating that into a more believable and fitting look for the Marvel Cinematic Universe was an enjoyable challenge. Even though [Marvel Head of Visual Development] Charlie Wen ended up coming up with the final design, I think I had the most fun also trying to come up with a look for Malekith."

Concept art by Andy Park (main); Justin Sweet, Andy Park (top insets); Andy Park (bottom insets).

Wen agrees: "As you would imagine, a direct screen translation of the comics design would not have fit very well into the Marvel Cinematic Universe. At the time we were receiving more specific direction on the Dark Elves, so we decided to put Malekith aside for a bit and devote our attention to them. If we could figure them out, we could take what we had done there as a base and further expand it for their leader."

Concept art by Charlie Wen (main); Andy Park (insets).

"One of the most iconic things about Malekith is his split face—white on one side, black on the other," Wen says. "After we did many different iterations that involved both full masks and half-masks, the script actually gave us the answer: It would be an injury sustained from battle."

Concept art by Charlie Wen (main); Charlie Wen, Justin Sweet (top insets); Justin Sweet (bottom insets).

Concept art by Charlie Wen (main, bottom insets); Charlie Wen, Andy Park (top insets).

"Malekith is the quintessential Dark Elf," says David White, Special Make-Up Effects and Prosthetics. "He is the same as the others, right down to the indented lines in his skin that trail down his cheeks. This is part of the Dark Elf evolution. They're born with the grooves in their skin, which are there to collect and channel the black fluid that runs around their survival suits to keep them alive and their eyes clear.

"I always create a logic behind the look, whether it's picked up in the movie or not. It's an artistic part of the backstory that is really important to me when I'm designing a character."

Charlie Wen concept art.

Concept art by Andy Park and Justin Sweet.

"Malekith has a grudge that goes back a long, long time," says Kevin Feige, President of Marvel Studios. "In dealing with the *Thor* franchise, we have the ability to play on these science-fiction concepts and these mythological concepts all at the same time. Malekith and his race of Dark Elves predate the universe—they are from an age prior to the Big Bang. They do not like the Big Bang, and they want to undo it."

Concept art by Justin Sweet and Andy Park.

Craig Kyle agrees, and explains further: "The thing that makes Malekith, especially, a madman, is this: While he could probably restore a single world and give his kind an island on which they can live peacefully and safely, it's not enough. He needs it all back. The universe was once theirs; he wants it all back. A piece is not a valid solution. That's why he's an extremist."

"Thor is not just a super hero," Director Alan Taylor says. "He has the weight of history behind him. So we needed a villain that had scale and was sort of epic, as well. Malekith and his people have been gone for 5,000 years, and they're coming back to—in their minds—right a terrible wrong. They're driven by vengeance. Basically, all Malekith wants is the universe."

Concept art by Justin Sweet and Charlie Wen.

Wen: "After I created the way the wound would fit into Malekith's face, I went back and refined the design to further implement the idea of 'battle damage.' For instance, the symbol on his chest is a puncture or blast wound taken from a previous battle.

"It was a simple way to tie in practicality with a design motif, while simultaneously creating the iconic and villainous image of Malekith."

Charlie Wen concept art.

Malekith face-burn test.

ALGRIM

"Algrim is a big Dark Elf who's Malekith's friend as well as his first mate," Charlie Wen says. "His silhouette is far more exaggerated than the rest of his comrades."

"Algrim is Malekith's loyal right-hand man," Andy Park agrees. "An intimidating presence among the Dark Elves."

Concept art by Andy Park (main, top insets); Charlie Wen, Andy Pa rk (bottom insets).

Andy Park concept art.

Andy Park concept art.

Algrim and Malekith are both long-lived, Craig Kyle notes, and have fought side-by-side for centuries. "Thor's great-grandfather probably fought these same men. To humans, the Asgardians may appear to be gods—but unless the Dark Elves are slain, they are as close as we'll ever see to gods. So even the Asgardians face forces that outlive them by great stretches."

Unlike Malekith, Algrim likely would be content with a planet on which the Dark Elves could live in peace. However, Kyle says, "he believes—and he's probably right—that the only hope for his people rests in the hands of Malekith. And if that's the vision Malekith has for his people, that's what Algrim will help achieve—to his dying breath. They are truly brothers in arms."

KURSE

"Algrim eventually undergoes a necrotizing and growing transformation to become the monstrous beast Kurse," Andy Park explains. "We didn't know whether this character would be fully CG or an actor in a body suit, so we were able to really explore the possibilities while keeping within reasonable 'human' proportions. His Kurse look is a result of him going through the necrotized transformation while disguised as one of the marauders."

Concept art by Charlie Wen (main); Andy Park (insets).

Charlie Wen concept art.

Craig Kyle: "If you go back to where these characters were born, in the pages of Walter Simonson's *Thor*, there was a great storyline where we got to see Algrim become Kurse. And although we manipulated the exact way that those events unfold for the film—as we always have to do, in the Marvel Cinematic Universe—it still rings absolutely true to the vision that inspired the character from the comics."

Charlie Wen concept art.

Production still.

"The transition to Kurse needed to be something visceral and frightening; it had to look painful as much as it did threatening," Charlie Wen says. "His breadth increases; his entire body feels more pointed and violent. We took the feel of the burnt-wood texture to the next level, extending it throughout his body. The marauder costume was grafted to his body, combining elements from his Dark Elf look with the marauder uniform."

Andy Park keyframe.

DARK ELVES

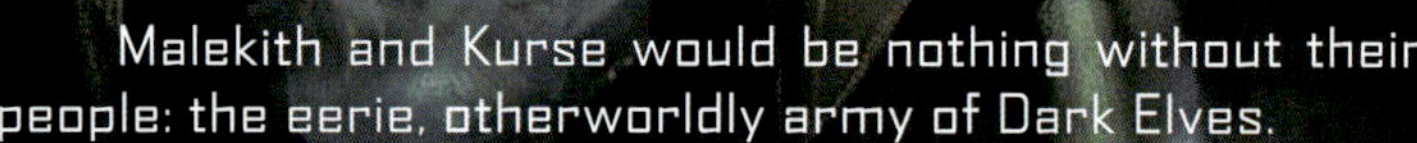

Malekith and Kurse would be nothing without their people: the eerie, otherworldly army of Dark Elves.

"Coming up with the Dark Elves' look was easily the most challenging aspect of the Visual Development stage of this project," Andy Park recalls. "Because we weren't bound to any particular look established in the Marvel comic books, we explored a whole gamut of possibilities—from the monstrous and organic to the more tribal and mysterious."

Charlie Wen agrees: "We naturally associate the word 'elf' with the realm of fantasy, and that was definitely *not* the direction we were hoping to take them. This is a race of survivalists and the last of their kind. We had to find a way to draw elements from the naturalistic side of 'elven culture' while crafting an alien race."

Concept art by Justin Sweet (main, bottom insets); Charlie Wen (top insets).

Concept art by Andy Park (main, bottom insets);
Charlie Wen, Justin Sweet (top insets).

"The development of the Dark Elves came in a rush of fevered creativity—the kind that happens so fast and clear, you can't figure out exactly how you got there," David White recalls. "Alan Taylor was keen to avoid using anything that is earthbound and recognizable, so no round tubing or buttons or zips are seen."

Concept art by Justin Sweet (main, top insets); Andy Park (bottom insets).

"I designed the hair for the Dark Elves, making it from a combination of synthetic and yak hair, all bleached white and silver," White continues. "I had Malekith and Algrim's hair plaited, which gave them a very regal and noble sensibility."

Concept art by Andy Park (main, top insets); Charlie Wen, Justin Sweet (bottom insets).

"Elves have been celebrated more and more recently," Alan Taylor says. "J.R.R. Tolkien had his take on them; in the 19th century, the Victorians had a whole thing about elves. Our elves are different. They are sort of refined and sophisticated the way we think of elves being, but they're really dangerous. There's nothing cute about our elves."

Charlie Wen concept art.

Concept art by Charlie Wen (left) and Andy Park (right).

"We utilized the textures Charlie Wood was using for the ships, a charred wood-like quality," Wen says, "and implemented that on top of the undersuit designs our department had created. This created uniformity between the ships and the Elves themselves."

White adds, "To create a subtly exotic and organic-looking race of Dark Elves, I looked at many real-life creatures: some that live in our deepest oceans, and some that exist in the harshest of environments on earth—like scorpions, micro-bugs, ghost crabs, etc."

Park: "There could be a whole separate art book for the iterations we came up with. Eventually Alan Taylor wanted a more mysterious and ambiguous, yet slightly sad, look to the Dark Elves. Thus the direction we ended up with, using the masks."

Charlie Wen concept art.

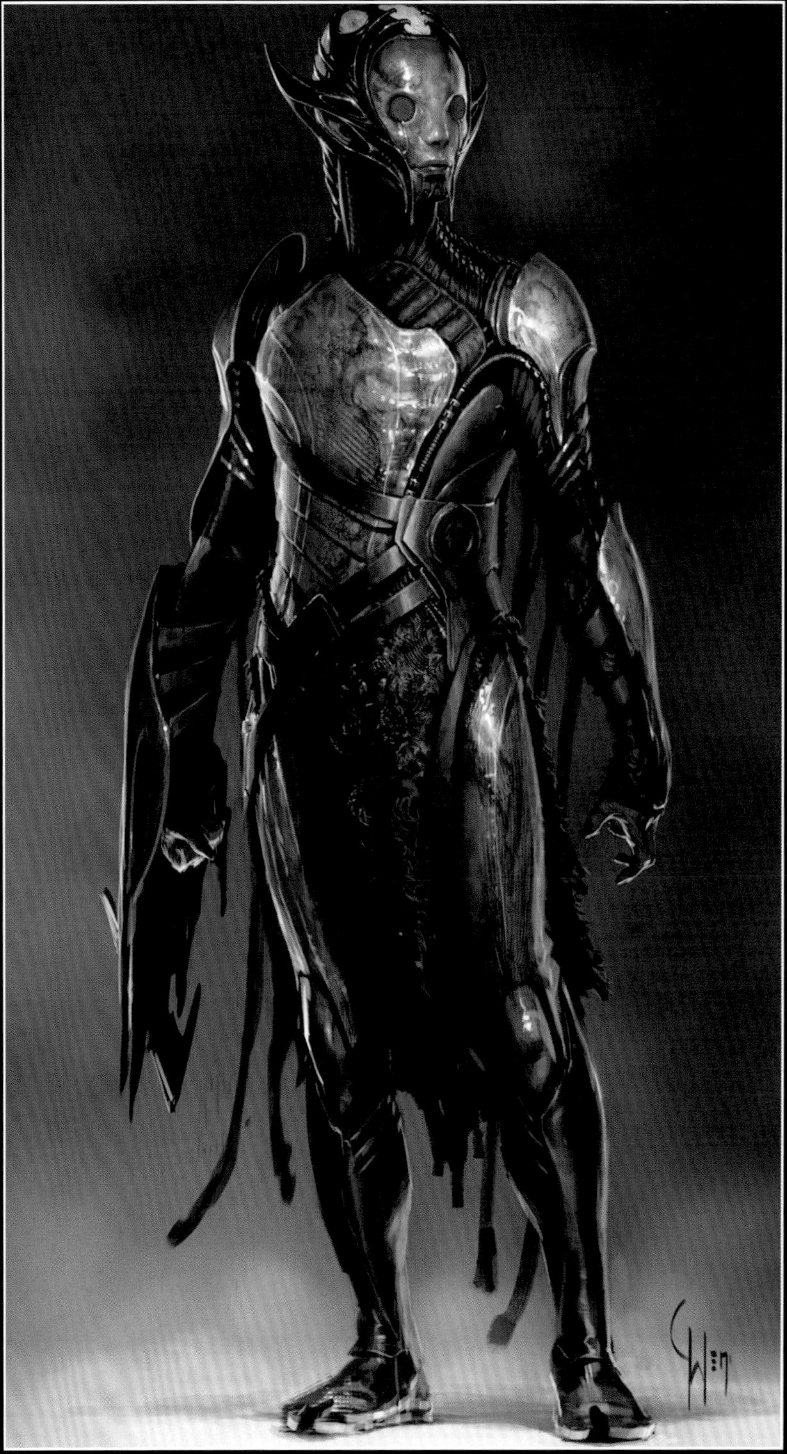

"Director Alan Taylor wanted to convey a direct contrast of beauty and elegance with the dark nature of the Elves' desolate and decaying homeworld, Svartalfheim," Wen says. "One element he was drawn to was the round, emotionless eyes on the masks. We did multiple iterations of the masks trying to capture the grace and simplicity that Alan was hoping to express.

"The pearlescent plating of the masks was the next step; utilizing a material that was pure further conveyed the juxtaposition of beauty vs. destruction. At first read, the Dark Elves look very pristine. But when you look at them further, you begin to notice that underneath the pearlescent armor is a black survival suit."

Concept art by Justin Sweet and Charlie Wen.

Production and behind-the-scenes stills.

Algrim isn't the only Dark Elf to undergo the monstrous Kurse process, which involves crushing a body-transforming capsule in the subject's hand. "In the film's prologue, we see multiple elves doing this in an ancient war with Asgard and its king at the time—Bor, Odin's father," Eric Carroll explains. "We did this mainly to set up the idea that the Elves only have one of these capsules left by the time the events of our film roll around—to answer the question of why they don't send in twenty 'Kurses' when they attack Asgard."

Blur Studios concept art.

Andy Park concept art.

DARK ELF WEAPONS

Dan Walker concept art with behind-the-scenes stills.

Property Master Barry Gibbs discusses the creation of this Dark Elf weapon: "We were given an image of the Dark Elf carrying a backpack, and then we had to turn that into a weapon. So the way we did that was to make it a foldout gun. Effectively, as you pull it off your back, you twist it and flick it, and the weapon unfolds into the weapon you see in the other images."

"At one point," Gibbs says, "we thought about having the weapon hurl a grenade, so that's what that light source is in the center of the foldout gun—essentially, a grenade that can be launched like a jai-alai ball. It can also be used in a slashing motion. It's really for close-contact work."

Concept art by Dan Walker (top) and Tom Whitehouse (bottom).

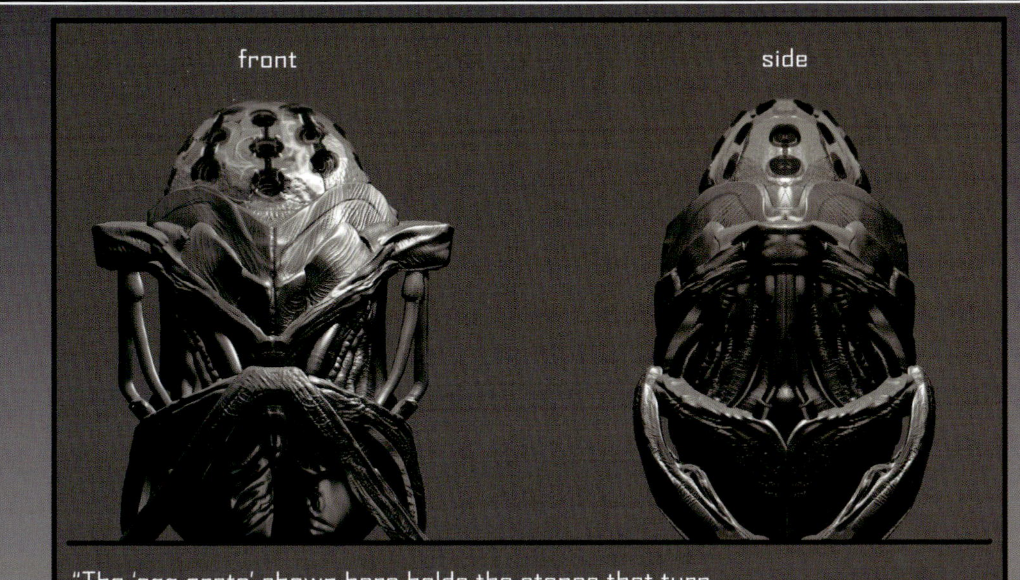

"The 'egg crate' shown here holds the stones that turn Dark Elves into the Kursed," Eric Carroll explains."

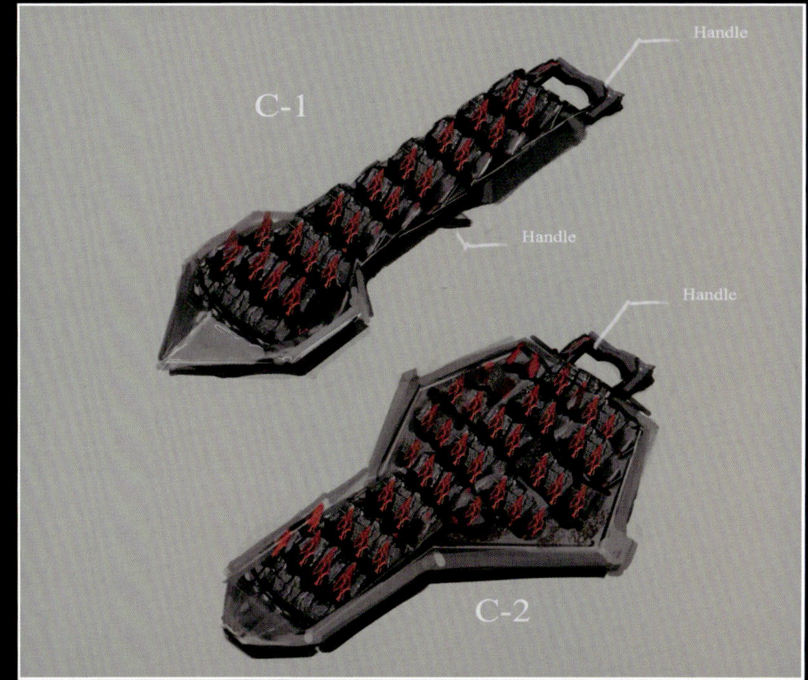

Anthony Francisco concept art.

"These are basically step-by-step concepts of how a lump of 'dark matter'—as it was described in an early stage of the script—was thrown at one of the guards," says Kevin Jenkins, Framestore's Art Director and Lead Concept Artist. "They were like personal dark-matter grenades. It was a way of dark matter killing the guards."

Framestore "dark matter" studies.

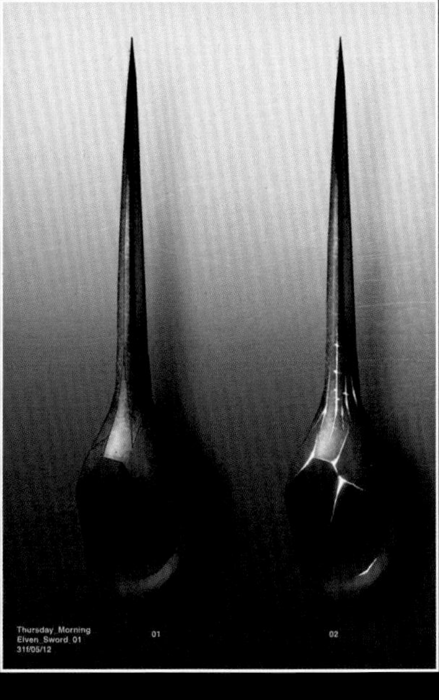

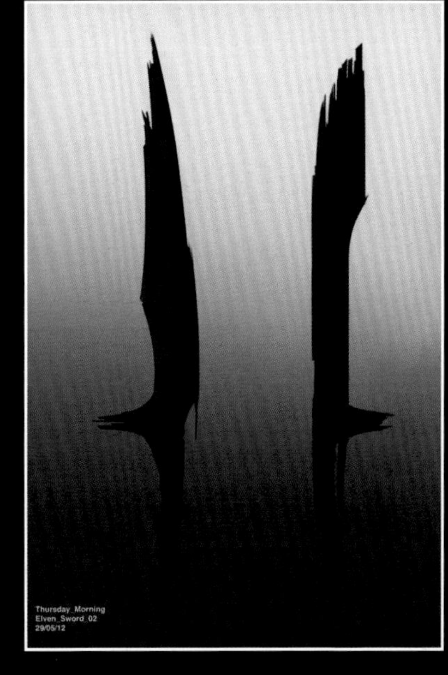

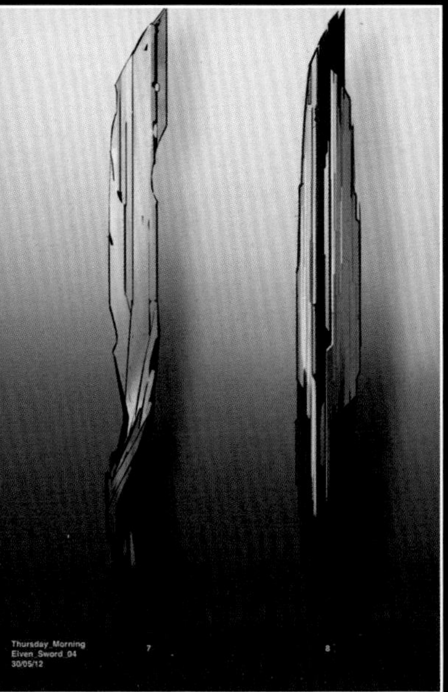

Dan Walker concept art.

DARK ELF HARROWS

"The Harrow ship was an interesting one," Charles Wood says, "especially in the attack on Asgard. We wanted a machine that could fly into it, and then crash into the Throne Room."

"The Harrow ships are the fighter craft," Cumron Ashtiani explains. "Unlike the monolithic mother ship, they are fast and agile. We had the idea that they hang from the underside of the mother ship like stalactites. Once initiated into action, they detach and free fall like a rock. But when their dark-matter engines fire up, they are able to tear off at terrific speed.

"We themed the Harrow ships on a number of things—bird wings and also ancient sword blades—taking our cue from the design of the mother ship."

Atomhawk Design concept art.

Atomhawk Design concept art.

Paul Catling concept art.

The bladed Harrows pose a true threat to Asgard's defenders—at least until Thor and Loki manage to gain control of one, as seen here. "The Harrows move incredibly nimbly, with two pilots," Craig Kyle says. "They use laser fire or blunt weapons. They're able to knife their way through the atmosphere and carve their way through Asgardian structures."

Production still.

As with the mother ship, the physical materials behind the Harrow ships were considered carefully. "We looked at bird feathers," Wood says. "We looked at crow feathers; we looked at the iridescent colors that you find on bird wings. All those things influenced us.

"We looked at the way one material overlays another on an armadillo, like a plating technique. There were lots of animal/geological/organic things that all came together in these vehicles.

"We realized that by simply flipping the Harrow ship from a vertical flying position to a horizontal flying position, it became a flying blade. That was a very simple maneuver that became extremely effective. We liked the fact that it had this blade on it that could cut through the Asgardian columns. It had this sort of dagger-like quality to it."

Framestore concept art.

SVARTALFHEIM

For the devastated realm of Svartalfheim, home to Malekith and the Dark Elves, the filmmakers sought out "the deadest place on Earth," Charles Wood says. "So we ended up going to Iceland, and working on a lot of the lava flows in Iceland. It's a really extraordinary landscape: incredible volcanic forms, ashen plains, extremely surreal.

"We have a scene where Malekith walks out across these bleak tundras and puts his hand into some volcanic ash, which was once a living space. And the light was so extraordinary, we could take full advantage of these fabulous mists and cloud systems that you find there.

"The great thing about Iceland is, it's an exhausting place because it's so dry and it's so windswept. It's a really stunning place to work. The landscape does so much, you don't need to build lavish sets. Nature has created all of that. Sometimes you find those sorts of David Lean moments, isolated and swallowed up in this enormous, vast nothingness."

Framestore/Kevin Jenkins concept art.

Framestore/Kevin Jenkins concept art with Jackson Sze keyframe (bottom inset).

BLACK HOLE/DARK MATTER

Svartalfheim's sky is filled with an enormous black hole, absorbing everything in its path.

"Early in the design process, we were still exploring the idea of 'dark matter,'" Concept Artist Nathan Schroeder explains. "We didn't have a grasp on how it worked, or how the ships used it for propulsion. This image was one of a series created to try and visualize dark matter, its relationship to the spacecraft and how it was reacting with the planetary environment."

"That was a lot of work," Charles Wood recalls. "Jake Morrison helped me a lot on that. How the black hole worked was: We looked at the launch footage from the Apollo missions, and some of the Gemini missions. At the moment of blastoff—NASA recorded all this with multiple cameras, back in the '60s—you get these extraordinary combustion moments. The rocket is just lifting out of its cradle and, for a brief moment, the exhaust is sucked back into the jet itself, through some property I don't understand.

"As with all the work on this film, we tried to base as much as we could on physical properties, real things that we could take as a starting point and then turn it into something else."

Nathan Schroeder keyframe.

AETHER CHAMBER

The Aether Chamber is the key to Malekith's plans: a tall, ancient structure pulsing with energy.

"The thing about the Nine Realms is that there are a lot of relics," Kevin Feige observes. "Whether it's a Casket of Ancient Winters or a Tesseract or something else, they wreak a lot of havoc."

Filmmakers were exacting in their construction of the Aether Chamber. "We went all around England and found natural slate/rock formations," Charles Wood says. "I'm really so lucky to have the kind of crew I can work with in England, plasterers and paint crews. They took a lot of silicon molds, and we made these absolutely accurate plaster molds so that we could build a structure that was completely and utterly minimalist, but had a very high-quality finish to it."

Bob Cheshire concept art.

Bob Cheshire concept art.

"The interior is many, many thousands of years old—maybe hundreds of thousands of years old," Wood continues. "Maybe it's timeless—you can't even put your finger on when it would have been created. And then we came up with the language on the side, a cuneiform language on the side of the great pillar that we carved into it.

"Alan really wanted something absolutely minimal, memorable—again, monolithic. Something that would, once again, echo the mother ship, the Ark."

Crucial to Malekith's endgame is the Convergence, an alignment of the Nine Realms that occurs once every 5,000 years. As the Convergence pierces the worlds, physics-defying portals begin to open from one to another—but early in the film, the effects of this unprecedented event on Earth are localized to an abandoned complex in London. Water from a rusty faucet drips *up*. Glass shards from a shattered window hang impossibly in mid-air. An old cement truck floats, weightless, inches off the ground. And looking on in wonder are three children who entered the warehouse chasing their soccer ball.

Special Effects Supervisor Paul Corbould explains the story behind this image: "Probably one of our biggest challenges was the cement mixer we had on a motion-control rig, which revolved in the drum. That was quite a challenging rig to get right. When the children first come into the complex, they see a cement mixer. The boy walks up to the cement mixer and realizes it's all a bit strange. He touches it, and the bumper of the cement mixer starts to lift and rotate as if it's in zero-gravity mode.

"The rig weighed about 22 tons and the truck weighed about 14 tons, something like that. And it was controlled by computer hydraulics, so we could match the moves each time. There were three axes on it: a rotating axis for the actual truck, a rotating axis for the drum that counter-rotated, and there was an up and down. It all went well, but it was down to the wire, time-wise."

Magdalena Kusowska concept art with VFX still (inset).

Magdalena Kusowska concept art.

JANE FINDS THE AETHER

STORYBOARDS BY RICK NEWSOME

In one of the film's eeriest sequences, Jane Foster discovers a strange object and is involuntarily drawn into Malekith's plans. "I think this is the fourth version of the scene," Storyboard Artist Rick Newsome says, "the main difference between them being the environment in which the Aether plinth is located. Ultimately, it was described to me as a kind of circular mausoleum, so I roughed out a very large one in a simple 3D program and took screencaps to drop into my 2D boards as backgrounds. The idea was that the space was a huge crypt, and that the niches visible in the walls held the bones of Dark Elves.

"After I got the scene approved by Director Alan Taylor, I forwarded the boards to Animatics Editor Coral D'Alessandro. I heard from Eric Carroll that Marvel was so pleased with the resulting animatic that he didn't think it would be necessary to take it to 3D previs—the action and storytelling were clear enough to forego that step. It was gratifying to hear that there was that much confidence in what we had put together."

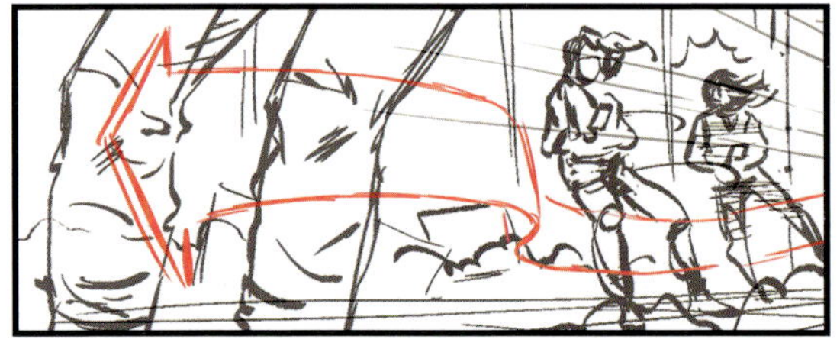

ARM GOES THRU WALL

RMBL

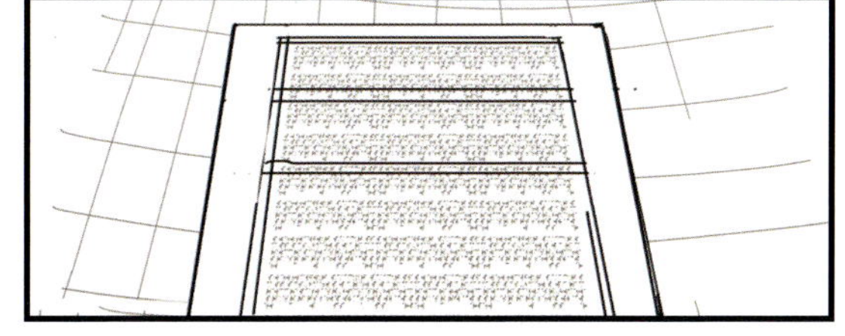

"I tried to maintain a variety of shot sizes, ranging from the very wide—to show the intimidating scale of the location—to the very intimate, as when Jane peers einto the space in the plinth. What seems like the smallest moment scale-wise is actually the moment at which danger is most imminent."

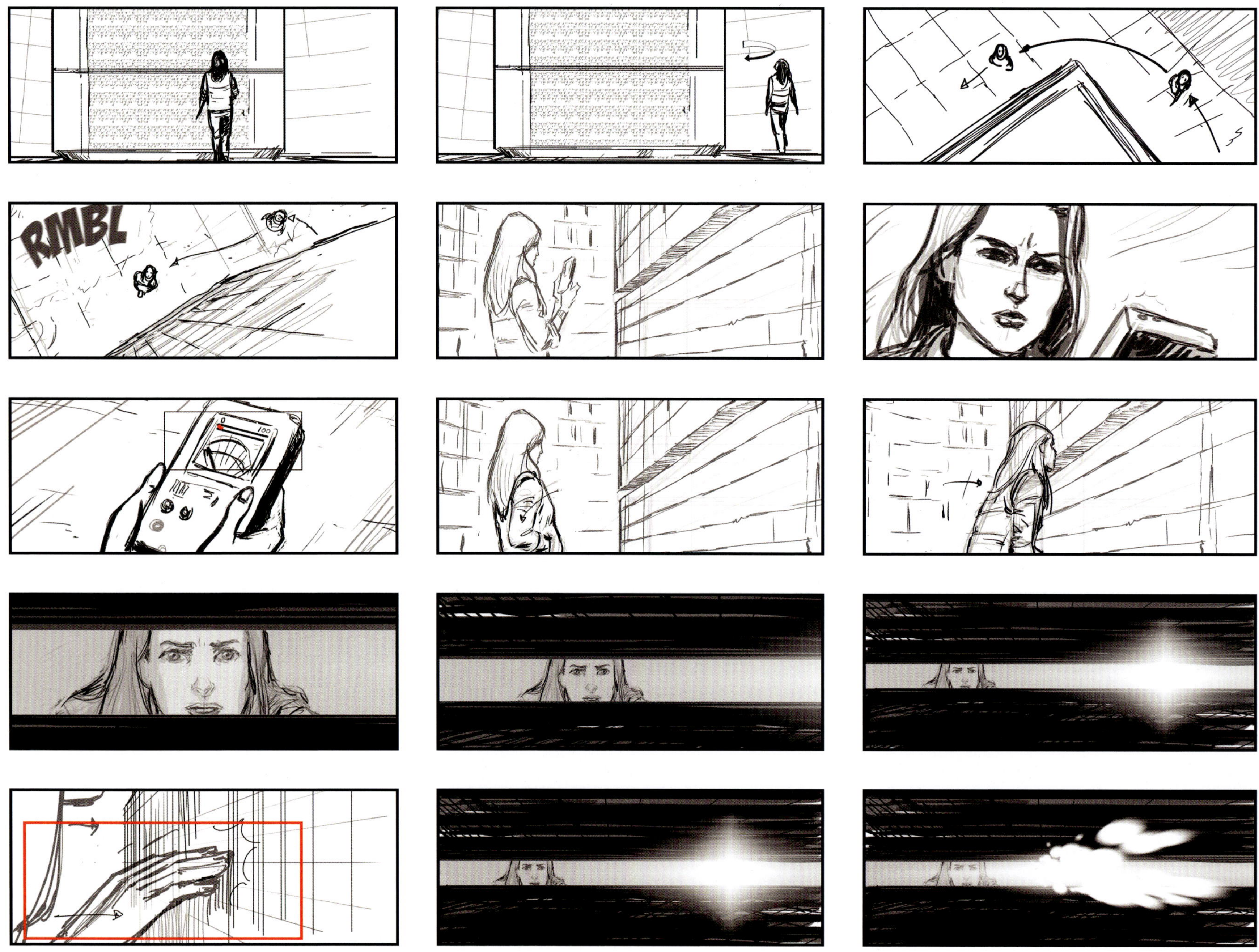

"Initially, the Aether was described as a 'black roiling liquid,' so I used a dark tone to indicate it spreading through Jane's body. I didn't much concern myself with what the effect would actually look like—I knew that the concept guys and the VFX crew would consult with Alan to come up with something cool. I was more concerned with illustrating the progression as it infects her, her reaction and the simultaneous arrival of the Dark Elves."

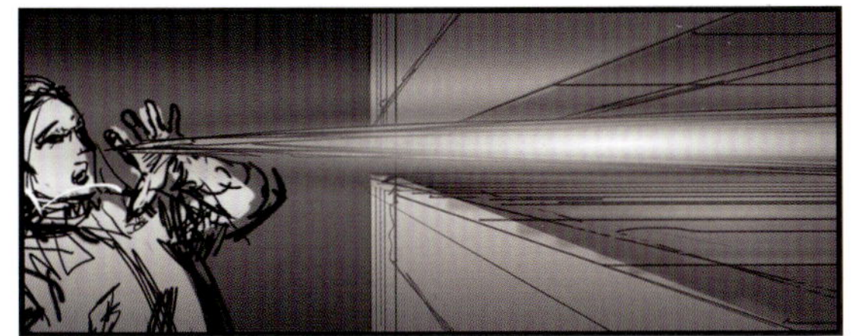

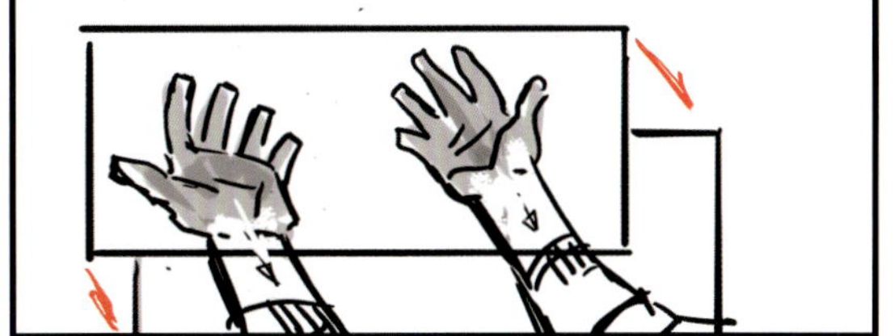

"It was more important to attend to the timing of the scene rather than try to precisely render the effects. Jane has to go from Point A to Point B and back again in physical space, but the scene also required her to shift emotions from curiosity to alarm and back again. This required some thought when timing the individual beats of the scene."

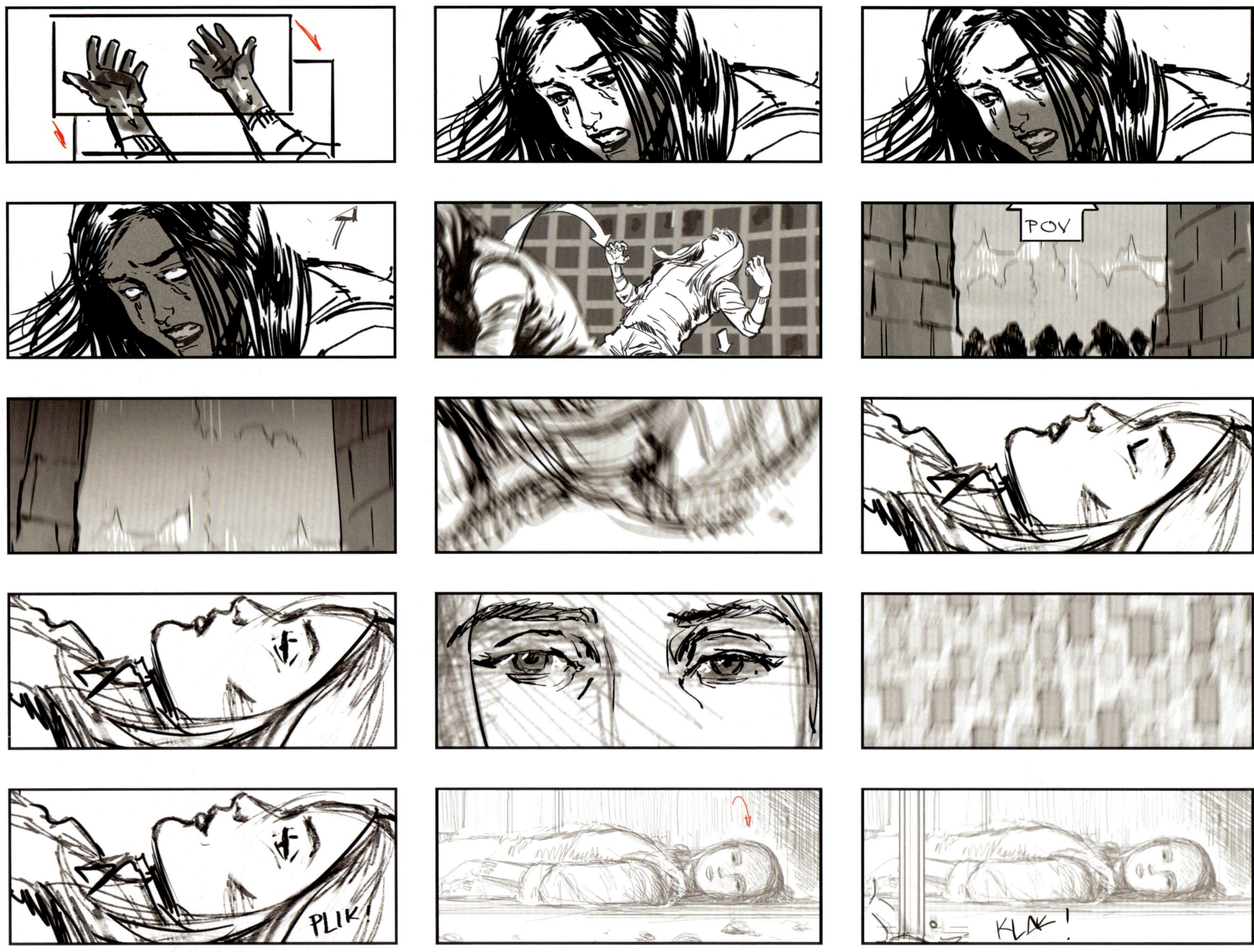

"I tried to keep the scene anchored in Jane's experience overall, particularly toward the end when the wall implodes and the Dark Elves arrive. Jane is completely distracted by the Aether engulfing her, in agony, so the commotion of their arrival is perceived as a hallucinatory blur of dust and noise. She doesn't get a good look at them—and the audience doesn't, either."

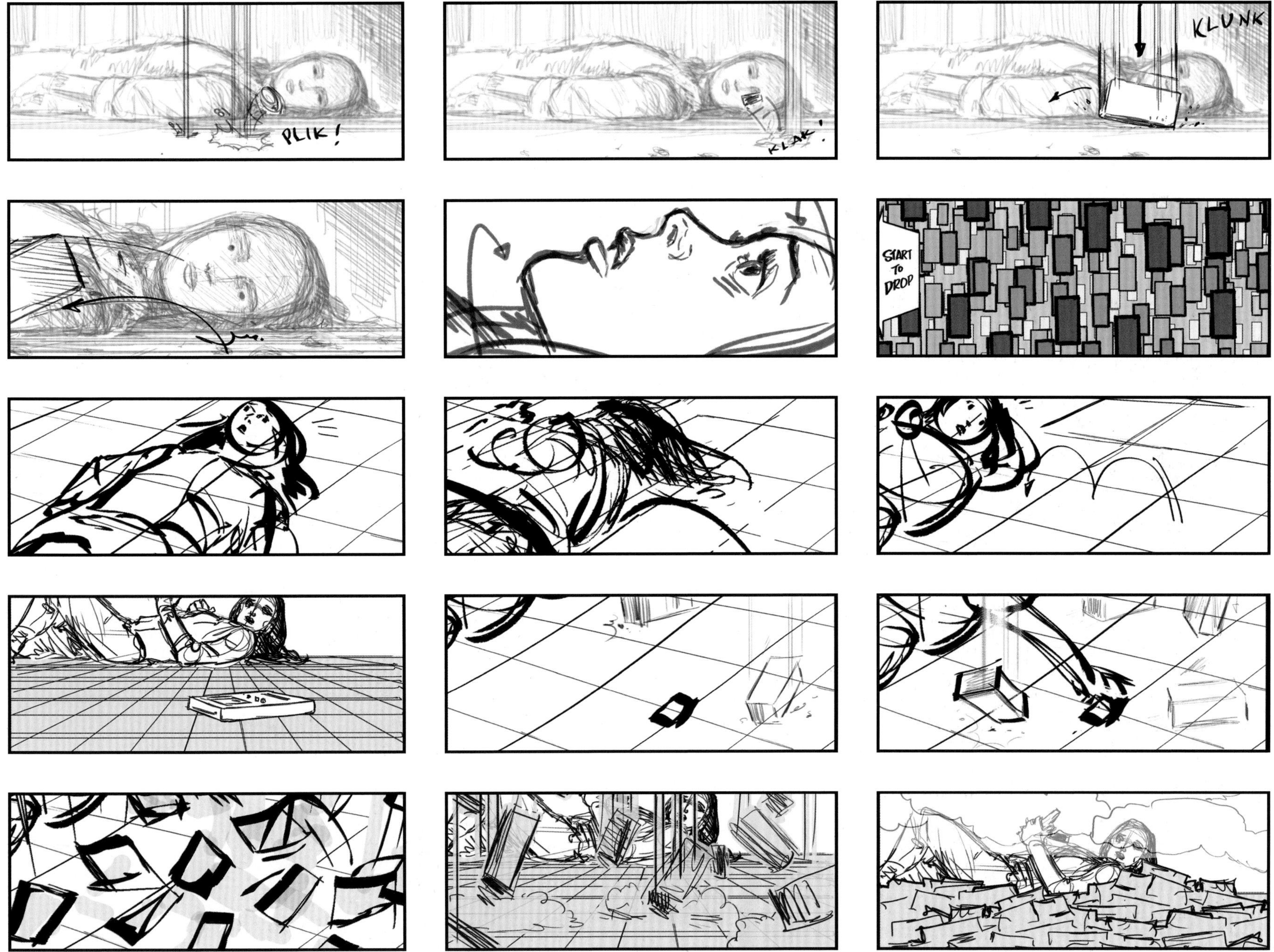

CHAPTER THREE

FOR ASGARD!

In *Marvel's Thor: The Dark World*, the filmmakers delve deep into the realm of Asgard—home of Thor, Odin, Sif and the Warriors Three. This journey required them to bring to life a wide variety of locations, including the Asgardian warriors' Training Grounds; the Chamber of Frigga, queen of Asgard; the undercity of the Medina; and even a Viking funeral.

"Asgard had been established in the first film," Production Designer Charles Wood says, "and what we wanted to do now was try and give it a sense of history. Since we had already shown the Palace, the Throne Room and so much of the royal aspect of Asgard, we thought this was our chance to meet the more common folk."

We encounter Asgard, its wonders and its dark secrets, through the eyes of Jane Foster—the charismatic, inquisitive scientist played by Natalie Portman.

"Bringing Jane to Asgard this time around, and giving a good reason for that, allows the scientist who's studied the stars her entire life to actually be on a distant world and even question whether she's still alive," Executive Producer Craig Kyle elaborates. "It's like, 'Oh, my God, am I dead? What is *this*? What is *that*?' It's just this great moment of wonder and question and fun."

Victoria Alonso—Executive Producer, and EVP of VFX and Post Production—adds, "The way we approach all of these worlds is to have a certain amount of groundedness, so they feel strange enough—so you know they're not around the corner, like you could take a 747 and land there—but they don't feel too far away, either. If it feels like people couldn't really live there, then we may be too far into the fantasy world, and we want to stay more in a grounded otherworld. That's a critical balance in the *Thor* franchise."

Concept art by Richard Anderson & Kevin Jenkins.

Framestore concept art.

ASGARD

"We wanted to see more of Asgard than last time," says Kevin Feige, President of Marvel Studios. "It's not all polished and golden in this film. We see the street-level view, the nooks and crannies of how people actually live there—real people, not just golden super-beings."

The filmmakers drew on many different cultures for Asgard's overall design. "Our influences were Norse culture, early European cultures—many of them," Charles Wood says. "There was some Asian influence, too; Indian, where we see the reflection pools and water gardens and vaultings and archways—a softer environment, so you could walk out over the reflection pools and then see this fabulous city beyond. Rather than everything being futuristic, we wanted to ground it in the past.

"But we tried not to make it just purely historic, either. We were aware, when designing these sets, that they would come in and add in technologies in post that we were unfamiliar with, into this more familiar environment.

"It's also full of elements. We wanted Asgard to have an atmosphere, to have clouds, to have raging waterfalls. The world of the gods. The waterfalls were dangerous, you know? We didn't want to tame this place. We wanted to make the natural elements ferocious, even dangerous."

Concept art by Richard Anderson & Kevin Jenkins.

Framestore/J. McCoy concept art.

"Asgard is full of waterfalls," Visual Effects Supervisor Jake Morrison agrees. "The entire edge of the planetoid is one massive cosmic waterfall, as the water pours into space.

"To make a fully CG environment believable, the first thing you want is for it to be naturalistic—even if it's a fantastical landscape like Asgard. Starting with a real place is always an advantage. I take the point of view that editing is better than creating. Nature is really, really complicated.

"Our Supervising Location Manager, Emma Pill, found us a group of islands in Norway, 120 miles above the Arctic Circle—so remote that it took three plane flights from London to get there! I've directed multiple aerial units before, and it's always worth building a few hours of scouting into the schedule. Everything looks different from the air."

Morrison describes the Norway shoot: "We shot about six hours of footage, a mixture of beauty lighting—shots that could be used as they looked in camera, with additional Asgardification—and, when the light was flat and dull, a massive library of texture reference. Motion-picture photography is really just a series of 24 photographs a second. So as long as your shutter speed is fast enough to avoid blurring the imagery, you can shoot a very, very long series of stills as you fly around, say, a mountain. A two-minute burst of footage will give you 2,880 photos!"

Concept art by Kevin Jenkins & Richard Anderson.

Executive Producer Louis D'Esposito notes that the *Thor* franchise depends on a careful balance of settings. "Some people will say, 'No, the Earth portion is the best.' And some people will definitively say quite the opposite. I love Asgard, the other worlds. We want to introduce realms that are exciting, that people can relate to—because if they feel like a fantasy, a made-up place, no one's going to relate. Subconsciously or consciously, they'll tune out that portion of the story."

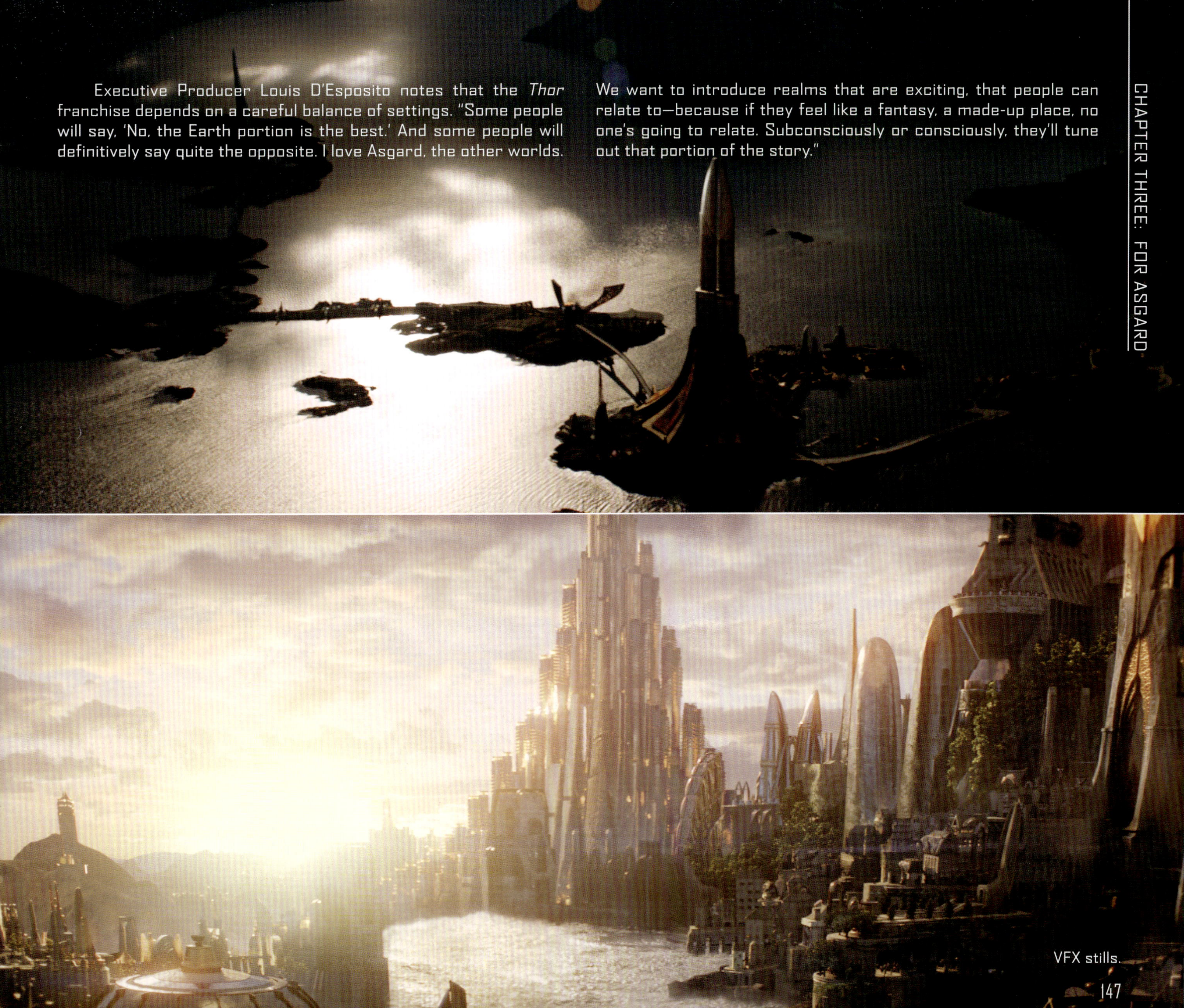

VFX stills.

JANE FOSTER IN ASGARD

At the heart of *Thor: The Dark World* is the story of Jane Foster, the Earthwoman who first met Thor when he crashed down, unceremoniously, onto our world. This time around, the tables are turned.

"Jane gets to visit Asgard—it's the very first time that we see a human there," Victoria Alonso says. "Jane is not only the love interest, but also has a special voice in what's happening because she's a scientist."

Craig Kyle expands on this concept: "Jane is super-smart, but she's got the long answer for these very simple and short theories that Asgard has. Things that we're still trying to put words together to explain, they just don't need to. For instance, the Norse believed that Midgard, Earth, was the center of the universe. We're saying, through Jane: Yeah, it is—it's the center of this cosmic cluster of wormholes that anchors these planets together. It's just a much simpler solution for them."

Bob Cheshire concept art.

Jackson Sze concept art.

Kevin Jenkins, Framestore's Art Director and Lead Concept Artist, describes the design process: "We did hundreds of pictures, trying to redesign towers and buildings. Because when we went back and looked at all the images from the first film, we were trying to add a bit more history to it—as if the city was built on top of other things.

"We also tried to redesign some key shapes and key buildings that were very Nordic in influence, because we had books of Norse patterns and stuff. So when the main buildings came along, we were looking at buildings in Iceland and Sweden and Norway—and even just the text and some of the scrollwork they did—and then trying to make some buildings that were seminally influenced from those."

Framestore/J.McCoy concept art.

JANE FOSTER

Jane's unexpected trip to Asgard allows her to trade in her usual Earth-scientist street clothes for some elegant, godlike robes.

"I had a lot of fun working alongside [Costume Designer] Wendy Partridge to come up with various possibilities for Jane's Asgardian dress," Concept Artist Andy Park says.

Partridge adds, "They wanted Jane to change into Asgardian clothes when she got to Asgard. There needed to be a separation between Earth and fantasy. It's a little like when you go to the hospital, you put on a hospital gown. But when you leave the hospital, you put on your clothes again. Because Jane's not well in Asgard, and is being attended to, the natural thing is for them to give her clothes that suit their environment and the comfort of their denizens.

"But though it felt like a natural thing for Asgard, it's completely against the grain for the character of Jane, who would never put on a dress and wander around the streets. She just wouldn't do that. She's too practical. What I thought was particularly lovely about the whole scenario was that she leaves Asgard in Asgardian clothes and ends up coming back to Earth in this frilly frock, at the worst possible moment in Earth's history."

To Craig Kyle, Jane's presence is crucial not just to the film, but also to the character of Thor. "She's the single piece of humanity that really helps Thor go from petulant prince to good man, even allows him to become a great hero.

"As for Jane herself, she was always the artist-scientist, a bit of a dreamer. She's someone who can see the big picture and is trying to find the clues to prove her vision is possible or true. Over the course of this film, Jane goes from the person who has had the smallest taste of exposure to the stars she's studied and loved to actually traveling to them and seeing the potential that awaits all of humanity."

Production still.

OBSERVATORY/BIFROST

As in the first film, the Asgardian Observatory serves as the gateway to and from the gods' realm, via the powerful Bifrost energies.

"Although the Observatory was destroyed in the first film," Charles Wood says, "I knew that the studio was very happy with that set. So rather than redesign the set, we decided to give it another character, an unexpected element. That's where we came up with this massive sky window in it."

Cyrille Nomberg concept art.

Cyrille Nomberg concept art.

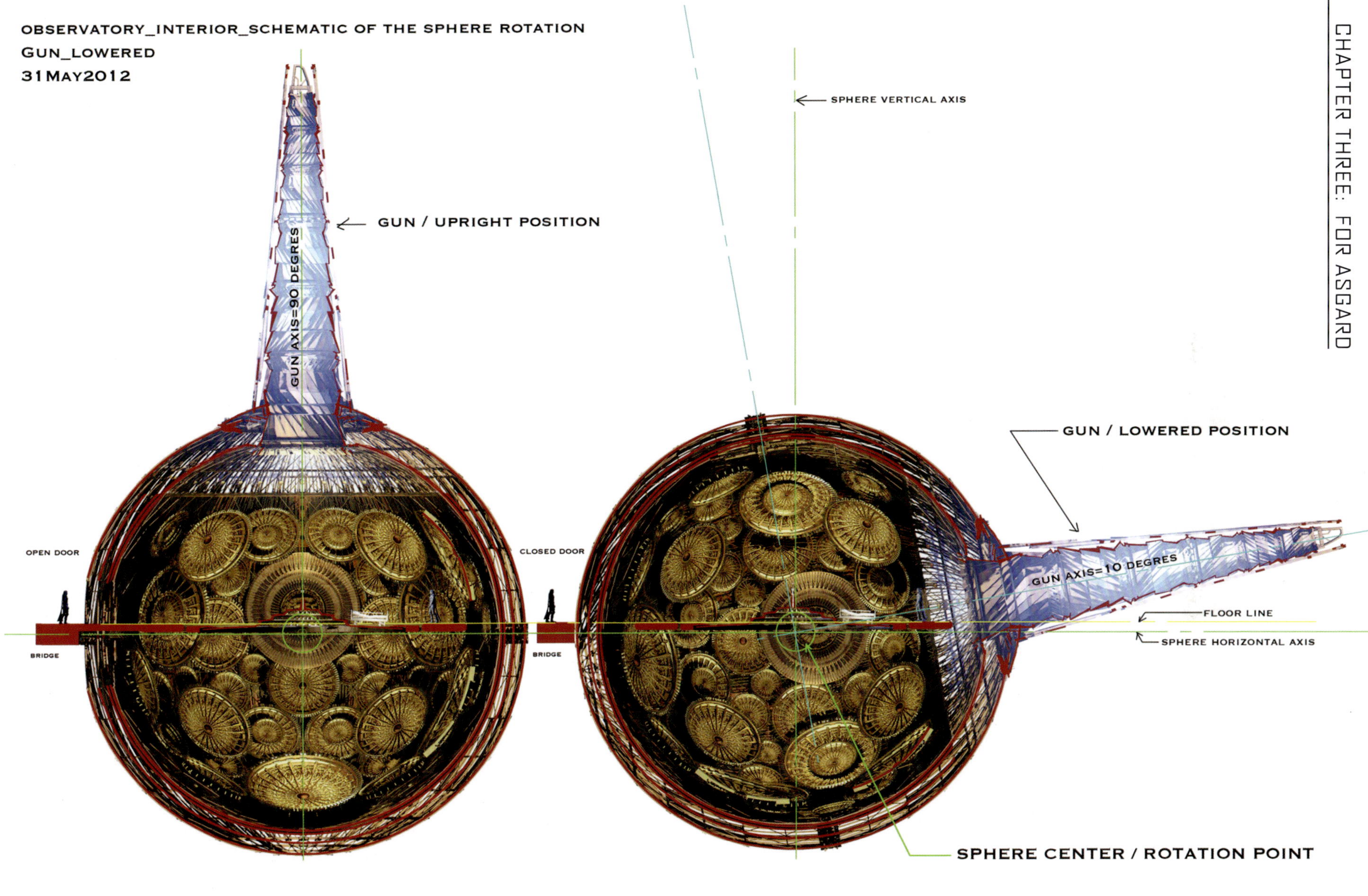

Wood elaborates: "As the Observatory fires, and it rotates, rather than you just being within a shell of something, now there's this enormous window that you can look out over the universes in. So it became a true observatory.

"That was great, having this skylight above us—where at any moment it could swivel around and that skylight would become a sort of crescent moon in front of you, and you could look out into space. Again, set against raging waterfalls, the mist coming up, all that sort of stuff."

Cyrille Nomberg concept art.

Cyrille Nomberg concept art.

HEIMDALL

Idris Elba's portrayal of Heimdall—stoic gatekeeper of the realms—was a standout of *Thor*, despite the character's short time on-screen. "He's someone we all love very much," Craig Kyle says. "Even before the film was in theaters, in the test screenings, people right away just loved him. So this time around we definitely wanted to build on the role he had in the first film and celebrate why people liked him so much. And Idris of course just destroys it.

"Heimdall has a helmet and design, like Loki's, that many actors couldn't have pulled off. But Idris wore it with such a commanding presence. He is powerful and honorable and truthful. And of all the Asgardians in the film, he's the only one who comes in about half a head higher than our hero. And that just feels right. When you are truly the first line of defense for an entire realm, you'd better feel powerful."

"Heimdall was the first character I designed on this film," Concept Artist Jackson Sze recalls. "The goal was to retain his silhouette from the first film while adding functionality. I reduced the size of his helmet and the original shoulder pieces, to make the armor more wearable. Also, to add function to a pretty exaggerated costume, we worked out his shoulder joints—clearly defining the materials, rivets and clasps. Heimdall also has twin swords in this movie. Their designs take after the sword he uses to open the Bifrost."

"Heimdall sees considerably more action in this film," Marvel Head of Visual Development Charlie Wen observes, "which made his look from the first film—big and shape-driven—far less practical in battle. Bringing in the shoulder pieces, creating an armor breakup in the arms to allow him to swing a sword easier—it was all about giving Heimdall a greater range of motion, while still maintaining his iconic façade."

Sze adds, "The tree on his chest is meant to be Yggdrasil, the World Tree that ties all Nine Realms together. Since Heimdall is the watcher of these realms, the amber jewel on his chest is the same color as his eyes. Heimdall sees all!"

Jackson Sze concept art.

Production still.

TRAINING GROUNDS

The soldiers of Asgard practice drills on the vast Training Grounds of the golden city, under the watchful eyes of the royal family.

"We come into this story two years after the first film, one year since *The Avengers,*" Craig Kyle says. "Odin has an army, which Thor is the captain of. Thor has basically been fighting with the Einherjar, which are Odin's forces, and his Warriors Three and Sif, trying to restore peace across all the various worlds.

"These are the best warriors Asgard has to offer, but they're just like any group that defends the peace. They are expert fighters, but they die just as the real heroes on our own world die in combat. And they love just as we do on Earth. They're the best of the best—but they're men and women, just like us."

Bob Cheshire concept art.

Bob Cheshire concept art.

Bob Cheshire concept art.

"The Einherjar are a royal guard," Wendy Partridge explains. "It's a little like having an FBI guy who is a plainclothes detective, and then the guy who's got the Kevlar vest on. The Einherjar, because they're protecting Odin and the royal family, always wear their armor. It is very stylized and very functional, and is intended to protect them in the heat of battle. Although the Dark Elves do manage to squash a few."

Jackson Sze concept art.

Carl Wilson concept art.

EINHERJAR SPEAR
HEAD PATTERN DESIGN

VERSION 2

EINHERJAR
DAGGER

BLADE 17″

Frank Victoria concept art.

ODIN

The relationship between Thor and his father—Odin, ruler of Asgard—spans a sweep of history, far beyond the confines of any one film.

After the events of *Thor*, "it's no longer the father trying to rein in his wild son," Craig Kyle says. "These two men have come to more of an agreement. The thing they have to tackle now is the changing of the guard. It's been five thousand years that Odin has held the universe together. It's a very tough family business to hand off, even if your son by all accounts is ready."

That power shift influenced Charlie Wen's approach to Odin's design. "In the first film," Wen says, "Odin was this supreme being, and his costume mirrored that. It was grandiose and full, from the billowing lower half up to the heavy chest plate and flowing cape. In *Thor: The Dark World*, we needed to show that Odin was continuing to grow older, and the torch was eventually going to have to be passed. As a whole, his look needed to be played down, while still giving him the appearance of a powerful warrior.

"I began by replacing the heavy metallic pieces from the first film with soft materials, like leather, much the way I did with Thor. Finding a way to integrate interwoven leather straps, along with implementing the iconic 'disc' shapes, further tied together the design motifs between Odin and Thor. Incorporating Norse-based knot work, much like we see in Thor's new look, was also very important to me. I was very thankful that these design elements were able to not only make it into the film, but also serve a purpose."

Asgard's ruler has evolved as a character, as well.

"Odin is called the All-Father, but he's one of the worst parents I have ever met," Director Alan Taylor jokes. "Thor and Loki are interesting because their father's so completely screwed up their childhood. You don't tell two boys that they're both meant to be king, but only one will make it! But in this film, we see Odin's character progressing. In a way, it's an interesting inversion from the first movie—where he was the rock-solid man of principle and certainty, and his son was impetuous. In this one, we start to see that Thor may be emerging as the stronger ruler."

Charlie Wen concept art.

Production still.

THRONE ROOM

As in the first film, Odin rules from a majestic Throne Room—and as with many of the Asgardian settings, it was subtly enhanced with added furnishings and a greater sense of scale in *Thor: The Dark World*.

"The Throne Room is still a big hall," Charles Wood says. "We wanted you to be able to look at Anthony Hopkins' character, at Odin, and believe that this is an ancient hall. This is somewhere where his father and his father before him could have existed."

Bob Cheshire concept art.

Bob Cheshire concept art.

"Every surface was richly embellished, and we used implied scale," Wood says. "Implied scale is a technique by which you just see the base of something. It's rather like walking past a giant foot. You build a giant foot—Poseidon's foot, let's say—and then because you built this thing that is thirty feet long or thirty feet tall, just by the very fact it's there, you can only imagine what's above you. But you don't necessarily need to show it."

Bob Cheshire concept art.

ASGARDIAN CANNONS

Asgard is defended by skilled gunmen in open turrets, firing cannons of unimaginable power.

"The challenge was to design military hardware for Asgard, a culture that is more fantasy-based than science fiction or modern military," Jackson Sze says. "We've seen swords, spears and hammers. But what does an Asgardian gun or cannon look like?

"Some of the early designs had shapes reminiscent of Heimdall's helmet—alluding to the fact that, like Heimdall, these are part of Asgard's defense. The final design combines a sword or spear-like blades that open to reveal a cannon. Movable components hopefully add visual interest to the turret in action."

Jackson Sze concept art.

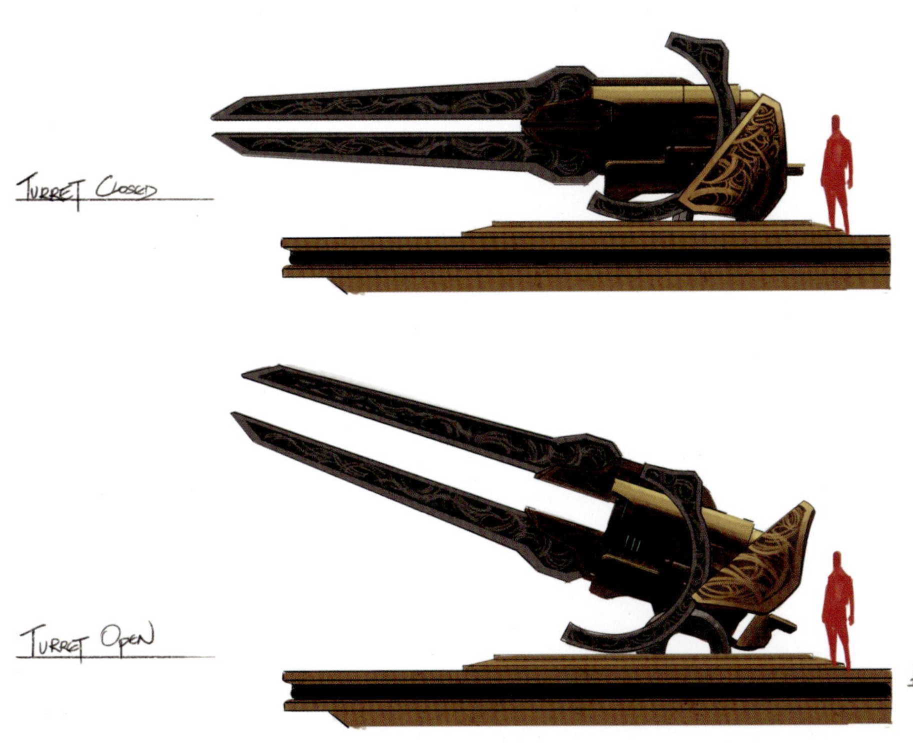

Jackson Sze concept art.

THE DUNGEON

Asgard has seen its share of rogues, monsters and even the odd Frost Giant. But no enemy has ever been craftier or more elusive than Odin's adopted son, Loki, played masterfully by Tom Hiddleston. In this film, we first encounter Loki languishing in a prison far below the shining city of Asgard.

"The Dungeon was something we stumbled upon in our concepting," Charles Wood says. "As we started drawing, we said to ourselves, 'Where would the dungeon be? In an asteroid, yeah? So could it not be at the base of this asteroid, can it be under Asgard? Why not?' We've already said that there's a Medina there, maybe there's also an ancient tunneling system that exists below our Medina. So we wanted to come up with the most ancient of spaces, the most forgotten part of Asgard, the bowels of this place.

"Another thing Alan Taylor wanted to do, which was really nice, was to have this ancient corridor and then suddenly within that to have these quite unexpected stark-white cells, with rich furniture and porcelain tiles within them.

"We tried to create a space that was very brooding and very dangerous—and then as the camera pans to the left, you look into this white-porcelain, absolutely sterile cell. The white of the tile against the greasy black-slate stone was something quite powerful, quite successful. We hope. We think."

Bob Cheshire concept art.

Charlie Wen keyframe with production still (inset).

"If the Hall of Science was the first structure built on Asgard, the prison was the second," Craig Kyle explains. "That black stone, the age, the damage—that was put there, stone by stone, by Thor's great-grandfather. And the only part that has been upgraded, since the palace was built on top of it all, is the interior. Because they found worse creatures, nastier threats out there, and the interiors needed to be strong enough to house the worst enemies that the universe holds. So the inside is bulletproof and far-worse-proof. The outside remains the same stone that the dungeon was first cast in."

"We came up with a set that was very, very primitive—very ancient," Wood says. "The darkest walls, the greasiest stone, the most crumbled world. Something that, again, was more like a labyrinth that could have multiple chambers coming off it—not dissimilar to the Minotaur's lair.

"So that was a wonderful thing to do. We used a lot of heavy stone casts; we used a lot of carving, a lot of Norse mythology. If you look at the film, you'll see a lot of surface detailing on the walls."

Bob Cheshire concept art.

LOKI

"Odin and Thor cast large shadows," Craig Kyle says. "It was easy for Loki to be lost in the darkness. But because of his mother Frigga's honest love and—before the big breakdown—Thor's love for him as a brother, there's a strength of good in Loki that he can't shake no matter what he wants to do. And that makes him a complex character."

"While Loki is in captivity," Charlie Wen explains, "he wears something very similar to his 'walkabout'/casual look from the first *Thor* film. The original direction from Alan Taylor was that his prison look could be what he was wearing underneath his *Avengers* costume. Unfortunately, as I began exploring that, we found it to be overly complex and cumbersome.

"So I used that idea as a starting point and simplified it, creating sleek and elegant lines that mirrored the idea that everything has been stripped away from Loki. He is barefoot and completely powerless. I also kept some of the design motifs we used in the previous films, including the interlocking wraps of leather and cloth that can be seen on his arms and legs.

"When Loki teams up with Thor, his power is restored and he is seen in the iconic outfit worn in *The Avengers*. This look, the one from *Avengers*, was actually the first step in taking the design of Asgard and humanizing it a bit. Creating intricate reliefs and textures on armor pieces like the shoulder and arm gauntlets allowed the audience to understand the materials on a much more personal level."

Charlie Wen concept art.

Production still.

FRIGGA'S CHAMBER

Thor's mother, Frigga, plays a crucial—if tragic—role in this film. Like her husband's Throne Room, Frigga's Chamber was redesigned to appear more vast and majestic.

"That was a highly detailed set that, again, had a lot of surface embellishment to it," Charles Wood says. "We didn't want to make it too complicated, but we wanted to make sure that the doors and the columns and everything were very richly adorned and, again, had a sense that the Chamber itself could be thousands of years old.

"We used reflection pools again—which was water, something we tried to use through the film where we could. The Chamber was designed as a meditative space where Frigga could sit with her son. Beyond that, we tried to design the set so that you could look out over the city of Asgard itself everywhere you stood."

Bob Cheshire concept art.

FRIGGA

"When we were working on the first movie," Craig Kyle recalls, "I often would say that Odin is the All-Father, ruler of Asgard, protector of the Nine Realms. But Frigga is even more important, because she's ruler of the Asgardian family and because of the boys that they have raised together. She is the glue."

For Wendy Partridge, Frigga's design was an extension of the work done for the other Asgardians. "In discussions with Alan Taylor, we thought up this form of molded leather that looks like armor/jewelry with these Celtic, curved, circular designs all based on a compass. The intention was for it to feel like jewelry, so it had to be beautiful. It wasn't meant to be like 'I'm wearing armor.' It was meant to feel like something they wore every day."

The sons of Odin often find themselves at loggerheads, but not when it comes to their feelings toward Frigga. "If there's a single thing that both Loki and Thor can agree on, it's the love and importance of that woman," Kyle says. "And her loss, we quickly agreed, would be the one thing that would allow the two of them to work together honestly. Once that debt is paid, all bets are off. But for the moment, until their mother sees the vengeance she deserves, they are absolutely both on the same course."

"Rene Russo was lovely," Creative Executive Eric Carroll adds. "She was an absolute blast to work with. There's a fantastic line in there where Thor asks Frigga, 'You still see good in him, don't you? You've got to give up on Loki. He's not what he once was.' And Frigga tells Thor, 'I didn't give up on you when you got banished.' Touché, Mom!"

Constantine Sekeris concept art.

Production still.

HALL OF SCIENCE

Perhaps the oldest building on Asgard is the Hall of Science, an enormous repository of knowledge built around a gigantic, ancient tree.

"We knew it would be exciting to get Odin into a spot where the all-knowing All-Father wouldn't know something," Craig Kyle explains. "If that were the case, where would he go to search for answers? He would go to this beautiful library that was one of the first structures built on Asgardian soil."

Kevin Jenkins: "The thing we were trying to do differently from the first version of Asgard was to have less gold and bling, as we called it. In this version, we were using a lot more stonework.

"This piece was partly done by Charlie Wood's Art Department, and he asked us to color it up for him. The color choice is mainly because we were using colder materials such as stone and things like that. We were trying to get the golden color out of the light rather than out of the material itself."

Framestore concept art.

Kyle: "There's a living tree that's connected to Yggdrasil, the cosmic tree—this beautiful cluster of wormholes that can allow people to move from one planet to the next, if they have a Bifrost. The tree shows the health and the status of the universe, so you can actually perceive Niffleheim and Svartalfheim and Jotunheim and Midgard and Asgard—they're all hung in the branches of this living tree. Should Ragnarok ever befall the Marvel Universe, the first branches to come down would be the ones of this tree.

"So it's a place that is special and holy and something that needs to be cherished and protected. This is a big side-story that people are only getting glimpses of and won't necessarily understand the history of, but that's what the tree is."

"The black-and-white images were explorations of what the Hall of Science might look like," Jenkins says. "We found some great reference of some old trees, and then we just started plugging them into the building. You can see the curves and the arcs and the shapes taken from outside pictures of Asgard."

Framestore/J.McCoy concept art.

The creation of Yggdrasil was both simple and rather involved. "We went out into a park in London and found this ancient chestnut tree—it must have been five or six hundred years old—that had died," Wood says. "We were given permission by the Royal Parks to mold it, and we took a mold of it and recreated it in the set.

"So all these root systems and such that are breaking out are all real casts of a once-living thing. We just wanted to represent nature accurately—and I can't do that as well as nature can, if you know what I mean. Nature has all the answers; I don't. So we thought it was better to go out and find something beautiful in nature, rather than us trying to do it from scratch.

"We actually reused the set for Frigga's Chamber for the Hall of Science. The Hall of Science was built around Yggdrasil. All of the realms are represented within the tree itself."

Framestore/J.McCoy concept art.

THE MEDINA

Thor's quest through Asgard takes him to parts of the city never before seen by mortals. Chief among them is the Medina, the lower city.

"What we wanted to suggest was that, within this city of Asgard—as there is in any city that survives millennia—there's an earlier part of it: the Medina," Charles Wood explains. "So we really went sort of backwards, to create a world that would show that textured history and a sense of time."

Kevin Jenkins adds, "The idea was for a tavern/street area of Asgard, where people essentially might go and get drunk and have a fight. This is a 'we're going down to that part of town for a laugh tonight' sort of area. It's definitely not City Hall. It's more the bar area where the life and soul is."

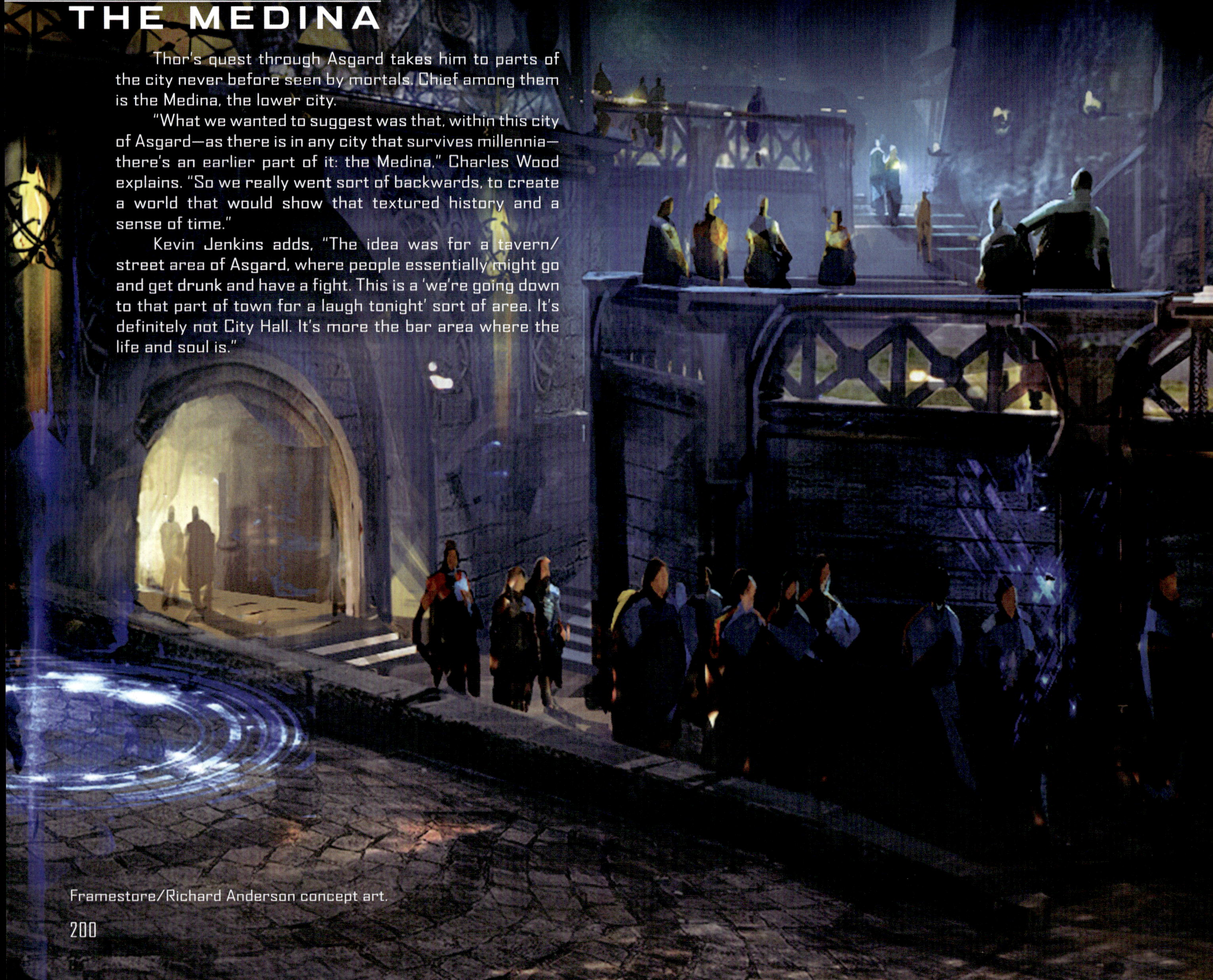

Framestore/Richard Anderson concept art.

Framestore/Richard Anderson concept art.

"When Kenneth Branagh came on board with the first film, he did an amazing job of visualizing the realms," Craig Kyle says. "He just really delivered the royal experience, the queen and Thor. We left understanding the royal aspect of the kingdom of the gods and the Golden Realm.

"But we didn't get a chance to spend much time in Asgard—to meet the people that our heroes fight for, that they love for, that they go back to when they return from battle. A movie only allows you so much time. So we held off on seeing the bars, the pubs, the stables, the city streets—until this film."

Production still.

ATTACK ON ASGARD

The Dark Elves' frontal assault grew out of the same instinct that led to the Medina: to truly immerse viewers in the realm of Asgard, on every possible level.

"In this picture, we wanted to see Asgard realized down to the street level, to actually be *among* the buildings," Jake Morrison explains. "In the first picture, it was all high and wide, and Asgard was a very clean place. For this one, we built some extensive sets and established that people actually do live there. And we also had, from the aerial photography, some high and wide shots. But what we were missing was that in-between where you're actually flying pretty low-level, in and amongst and around the buildings. The attack on Asgard was dreamed up as an exciting opportunity to go into a dogfight."

"This image was a keyframe that had been suggested by the storyboards," Concept Artist Nathan Schroeder says. "As the full-scale alien assault is under way, we see one of the large ships towering overhead. Basically, we are trying to establish a sense of scale and destructive potential."

Nathan Schroeder concept art.

"We follow these Harrow ships as they head straight in toward the palace," Morrison says. "And it's kind of like a cool, old-school ride film where it takes you on the journey. Very visceral—we get to see the Einherjar guards in their militarized flying skiffs, which have these awesome hunter-seeker missiles. They've got Gatling guns and cool wings that kind of fold back when they fly at speed.

"It was really a good opportunity to set up the Asgardians and the Einherjar guards as a little bit more powerful and a threat. You don't want to feel like the Elves have all the cool tech, just because they have a couple of different types of guns and they've got black-hole weapons. And we don't want to make it so the Einherjar really just have the equivalent of bows and arrows. So the Asgardians have got aerial technology; they've got flying skiffs with weapons."

Bob Cheshire concept art.

"This is a particularly brooding image," Schroeder notes. "We were looking to create an iconic image of Asgard under attack from the aliens, contrasting the utopian elegance of Odin's tower with the sinewy malevolence of the alien ship."

"The Asgardians put up a great fight," Craig Kyle says, "especially Heimdall, who does amazing damage to one ship just by himself. But they're caught off-guard, and it's that sneak attack that gives the Dark Elves the advantage and allows them to cut all the way to the heart of the kingdom."

Nathan Schroeder concept art.

"From the design point of view, we're using the same Asgard layout as we were before," Morrison says. "But the layout that you could use from the air, with fairly simple buildings, but enhanced using paint—what we call digital matte paintings—really wouldn't hold up for any of these shots. Because you're doing a dogfight down the equivalent of Fifth Avenue, going in and out among the buildings, all these really elaborate Jack Kirby-style crazy Asgard buildings with all sorts of holes and loops and things—we just grabbed all those and ran with them."

Atomhawk Design concept art.

THRONE ROOM CRASH

ANIMATIC/PREVIS BY THE THIRD FLOOR

The siege of Asgard culminates in a dramatic assault on the Throne Room itself. "The Throne Room Crash was one of the first sequences we previsualized," says Gerardo Ramirez, The Third Floor's Previsualization Supervisor. "When we started, the scene only existed as a few lines in the script; there were no storyboards.

"Working closely with the Visual Effects Supervisor, our team depicted the entire action from when the ship hits the first column to when it comes to a complete stop. We then placed cameras throughout the animated previs to find the most interesting and exciting angles of the crash."

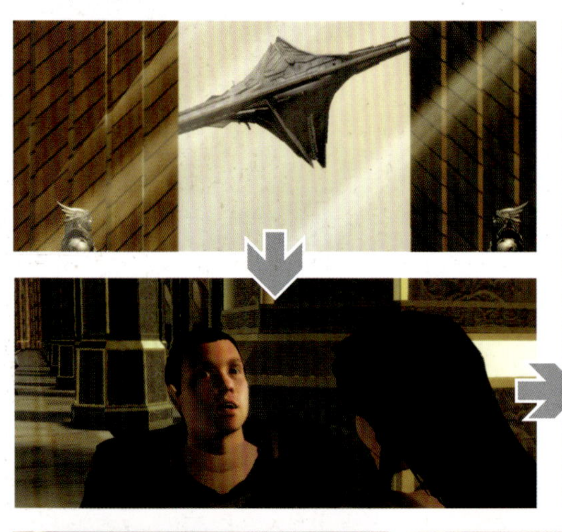

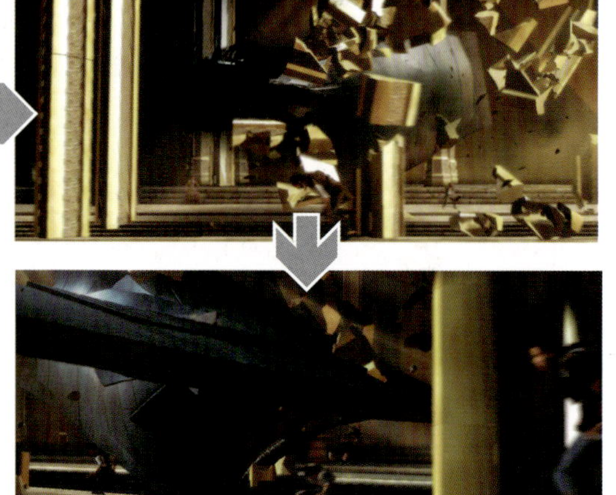

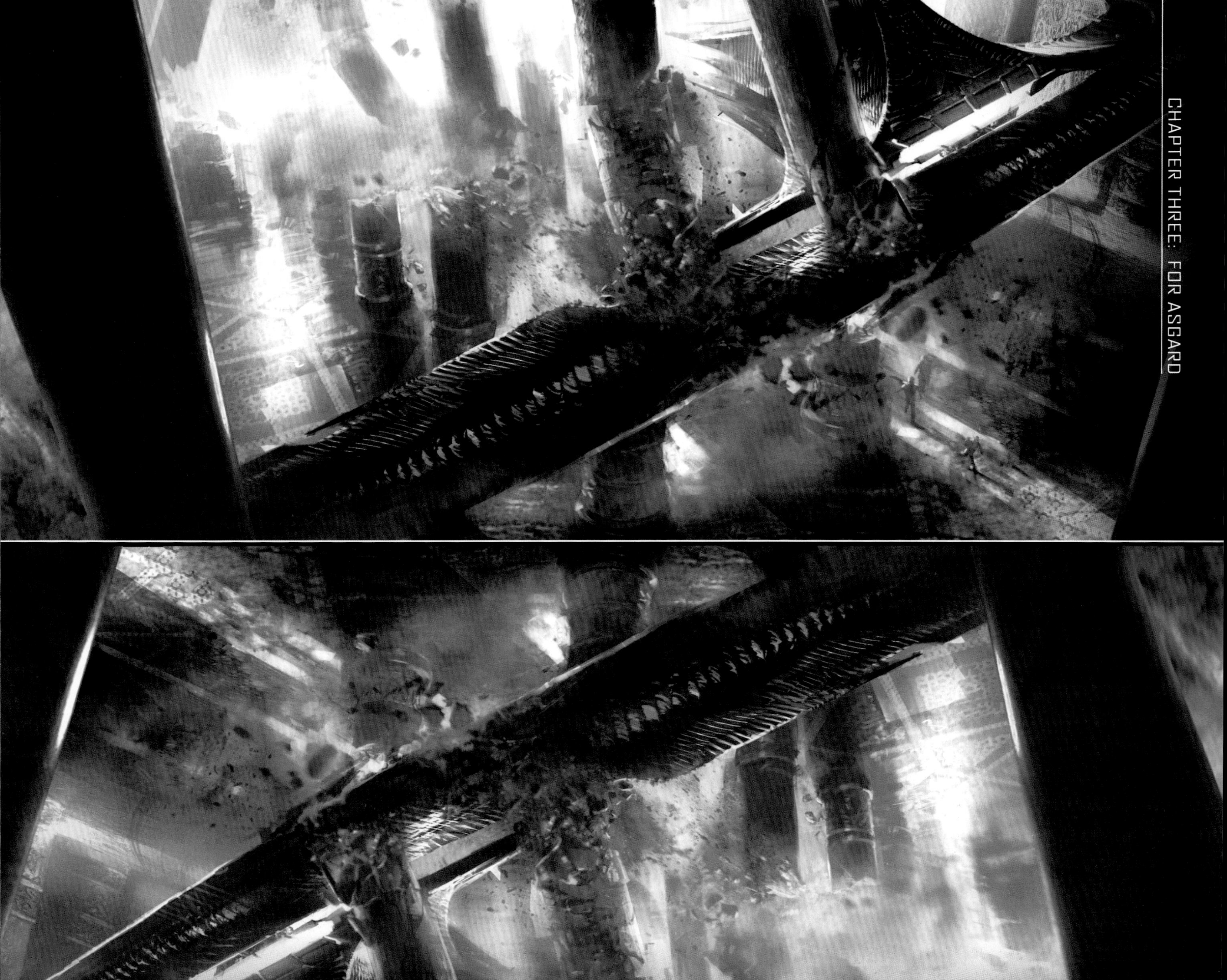

Atomhawk Design concept art.

Atomhawk Design concept art.

Atomhawk Design concept art.

Jackson Sze concept art.

"The idea here was to throw the normally grand and beautiful Asgard into chaos when the Dark Elves attack," Jackson Sze says.

THE DEATH OF FRIGGA
STORYBOARDS BY JANE WU

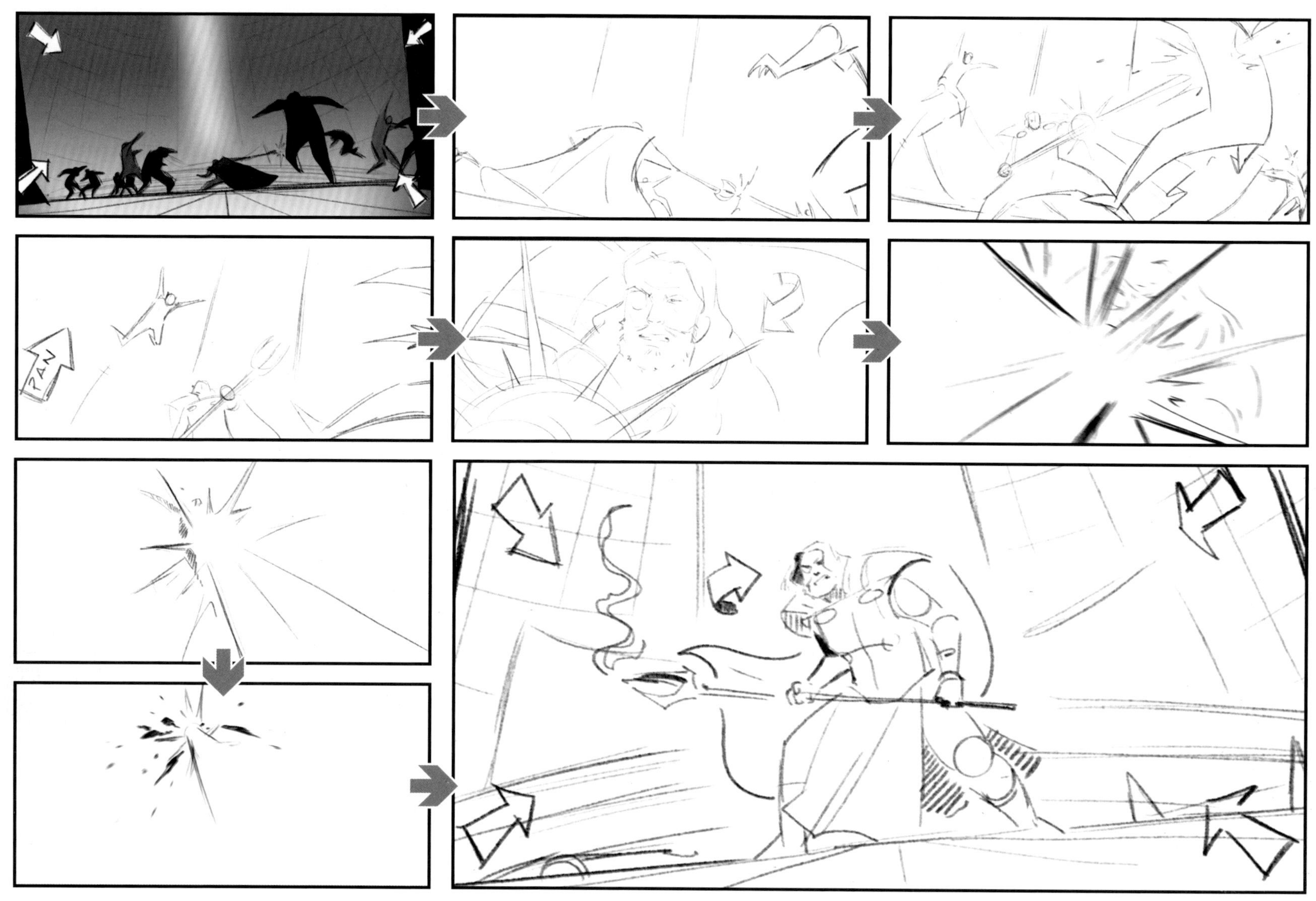

As Malekith and the Dark Elves take their battle to Asgard, tragedy strikes the royal family.

"I was grateful and anxious to have been assigned this important sequence," Storyboard Artist Jane Wu says. "This was a scene that illustrated the main theme in the movie. The biggest issue I encountered was getting the beats of Frigga's death, Odin's reaction and Thor's entrance properly told. When beats play out so closely, we risk the story feeling lost or muddled. The director was very collaborative and gracious in letting me try different ideas to clarify these issues."

Production still.

"This sequence occurs in the middle of a siege by the Dark Elves," Wu explains. "Odin is doing his part in the fight when he realizes the enemy is not looking for a surrender, but for the Aether. Malekith tries to retrieve the Aether only to be met by a formidable Frigga. They fight, but Frigga is no match for him, and even Odin is forced to lay down his weapon in an effort to save Frigga's life. This doesn't end well, as Kurse kills Frigga anyway.

"In that moment, lightning scars Malekith's face and the villains barely escape, as Thor belatedly arrives."

Production still.

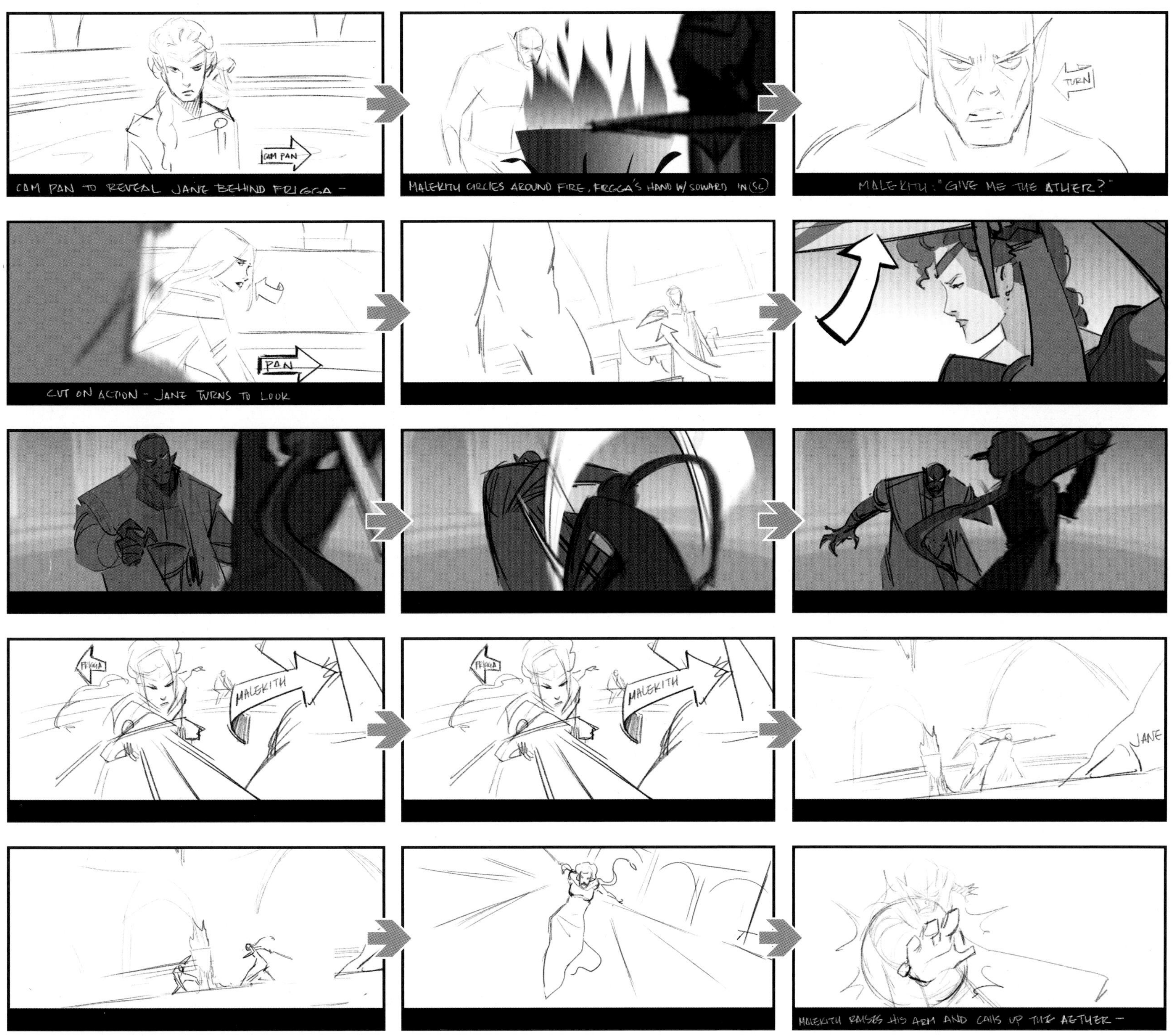

CAM PAN
CAM PAN TO REVEAL JANE BEHIND FRIGGA –
MALEKITH CIRCLES AROUND FIRE, FRIGGA'S HAND W/ SOWARD IN (SC)
TURN
MALEKITH: "GIVE ME THE ATHER?"
PAN
CUT ON ACTION – JANE TURNS TO LOOK
FRIGGA
MALEKITH
FRIGGA
MALEKITH
JANE
MALEKITH RAISES HIS ARM AND CALLS UP THE AETHER –

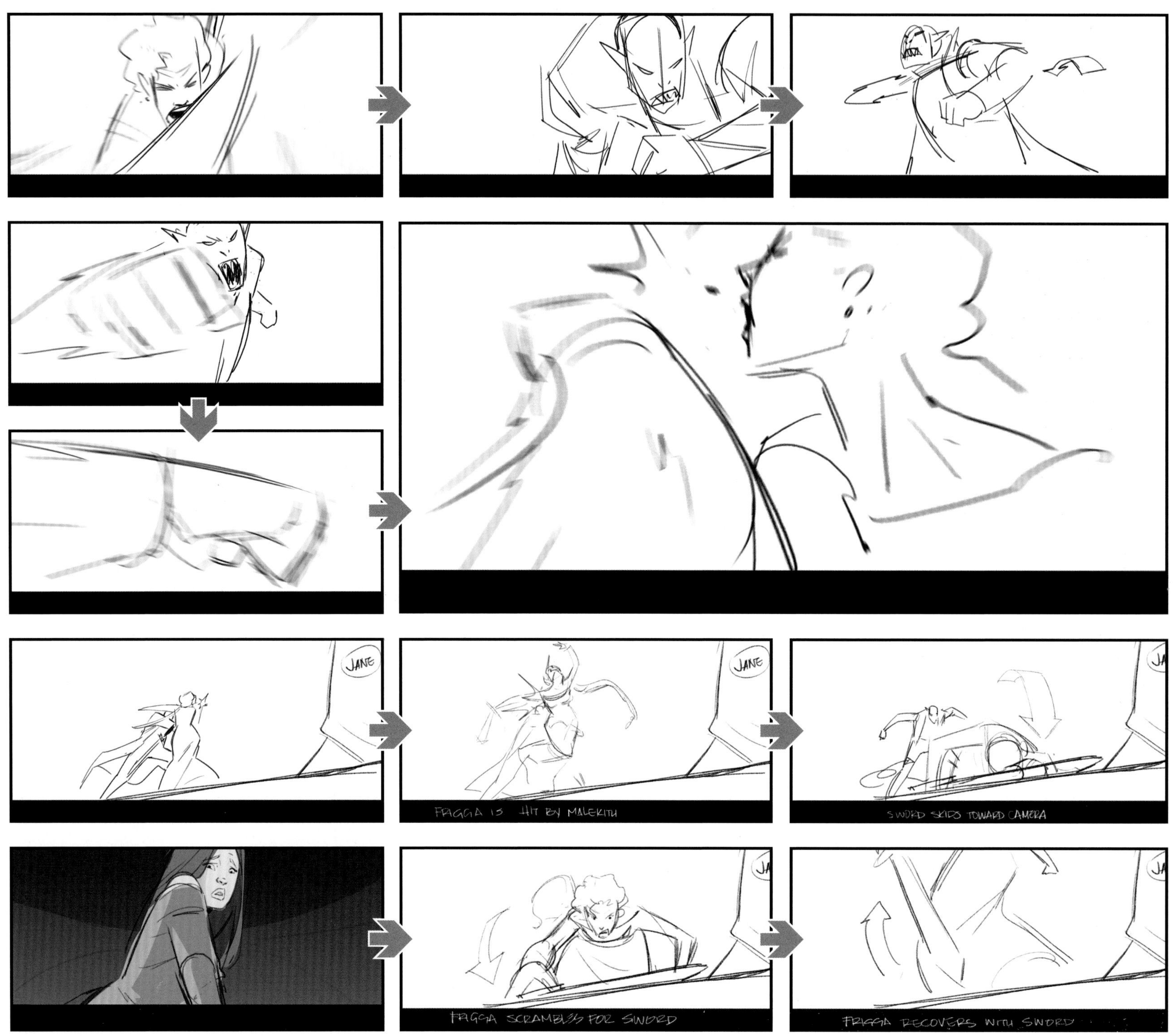
JANE
JANE
FRIGGA IS HIT BY MALEKITH
SWORD SKIDS TOWARD CAMERA
FRIGGA SCRAMBLES FOR SWORD
FRIGGA RECOVERS WITH SWORD

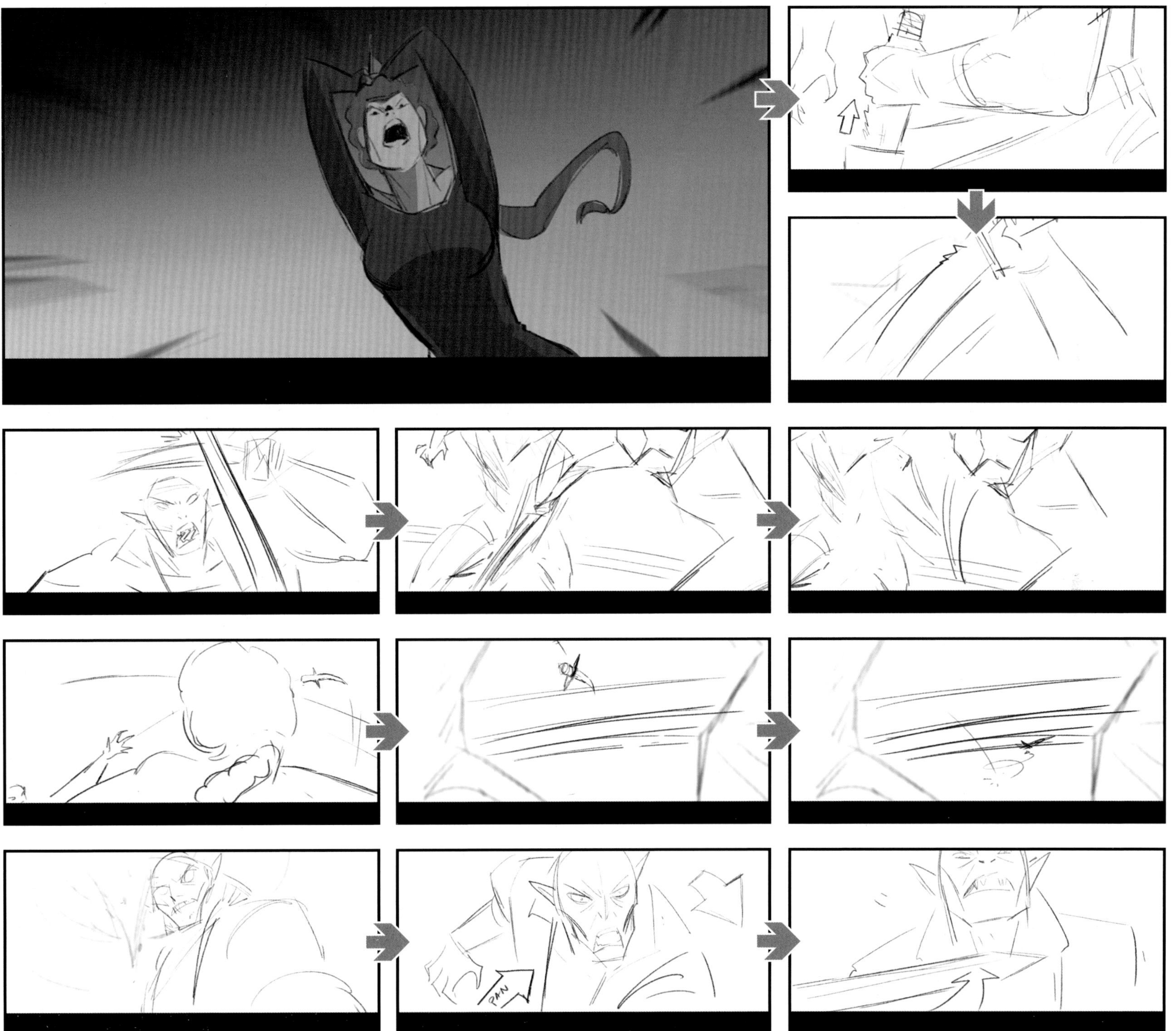
PAN

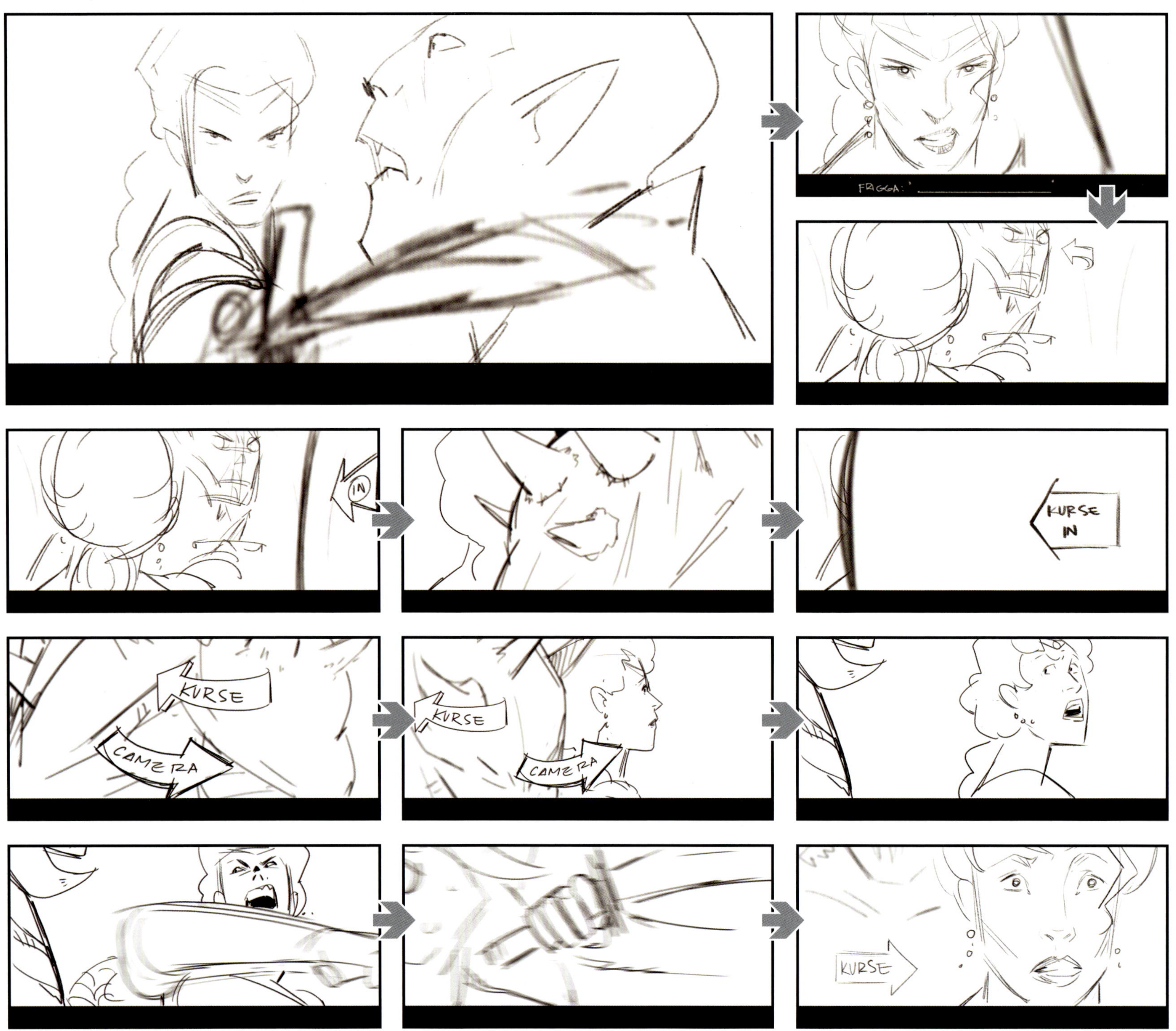

IN
KURSE
IN
KURSE
CAMERA
KURSE
CAMERA
KURSE

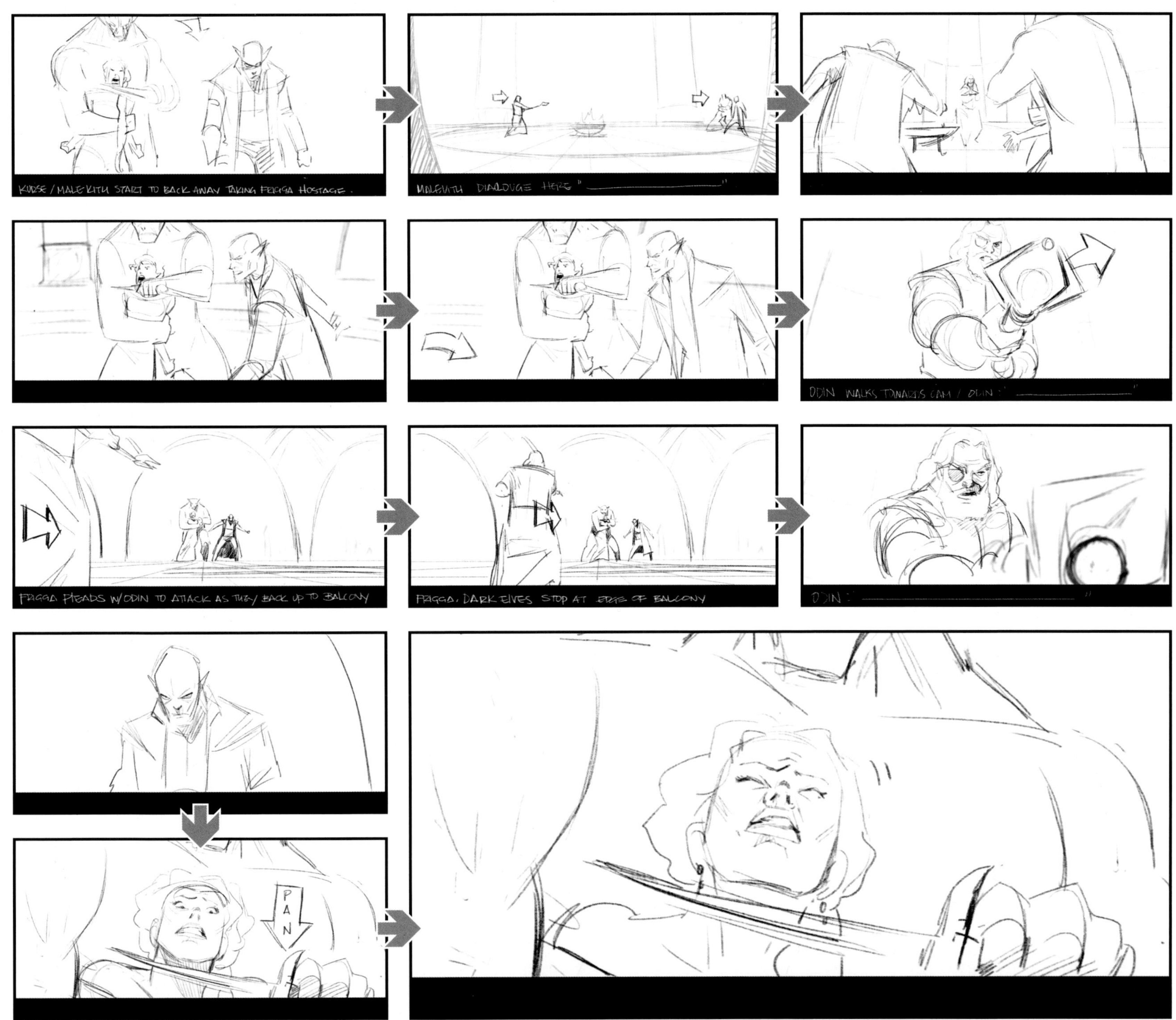
KURSE / MALEKITH START TO BACK AWAY TAKING FRIGGA HOSTAGE.
MALEKITH DIALOUGE HERE " "
ODIN WALKS TOWARDS CAM / ODIN: " "
FRIGGA PLEADS W/ODIN TO ATTACK AS THEY BACK UP TO BALCONY
FRIGGA, DARK ELVES STOP AT EDGE OF BALCONY
ODIN: " "
PAN

"The idea of this sequence was to show how vulnerable Odin was at the moment when he saw his queen in harm's way," Wu says. "I was also trying to create tension between the characters and show the urgency of the situation.

"This sequence also shows our most godlike characters experiencing the most basic human response: fear. Once Thor has injured and chased the Dark Elves away, he is left to witness his mother's death and his father's decline."

Production still.

SLIGHT DOLLY
SLIGHT DOLLY
CONT SLIGHT DOLLY

FRIGGA'S FUNERAL

Possibly the darkest scene in *Thor: The Dark World* is the funeral for Frigga, mother of Thor. The hearts of two gods are broken, and the soul of a third is sent to her ancestors in a fiery, ancient ceremony.

"Originally, we were going to do this massive funeral scene with the longboats, with her body laid out in it," Charles Wood says. "Then we ended up doing it in the Training Ground instead.

"I would describe it as a very elemental, spiritual, evocative scene. Very sad. We looked at a lot of different types of funerals from many cultures. You look at the Native American Indians, how their dead are buried; at the Hindu culture, the way they cremate people; how those very somber and sobering events in different cultures happen. All those things influenced this scene."

"We knew from the first draft of the script that Frigga would die in this movie," says Jackson Sze, who created much of the early conceptual art for the scene. "This is a substantial story point, and will affect Asgard forever. Several scenarios were explored with regards to Frigga's final resting place. We explored an actual tomb, an impossibly still mirror lake and the highest mountain peaks of Asgard.

"We ended up drawing from Nordic funeral rituals. Asgard is surrounded by water, so it felt appropriate. I imagined Frigga to be loved by all, and her passing would bring out all of Asgard to mourn her."

Jackson Sze keyframe.

In drawing on the traditions of the ancient Norse people, Wood notes, "It was a very warlike culture, but it was also a very meditative culture. Farming, all of those things that were developed at that time—in the 9th, 10th and 11th centuries—are still relevant today. There's a simplicity to that, which is true to the film, as well.

"Of course, we have such complexities as the Observatory and all the advanced technology involved, as well. But we were trying to balance those wonderful magical things against something less involved, simpler—and yet more majestic, I suppose."

Kevin Jenkins recalls creating several early renditions of this scene, seen from various angles. In this piece, "We had two long platforms, and then I did this very Nordic boat burning. It would sail between all the population of Asgard as it headed out—again using that motif of very fluted, flowing pillars that you see in some of our other buildings. I also did versions where the walls were closed in and the pillars were bigger or smaller or missing."

Framestore/Kevin Jenkins concept art.

"We built a set in Longcross Studios, almost like a balcony set with two massive columns, because the idea is that all of Asgard is mourning Frigga," Jake Morrison recalls. "So you have a good number of people, a big crowd, there. It's a central place to stage—it's almost like the royal box for the funeral—and we got coverage of our actors in full regalia arriving and then observing the scene."

"Throughout this film," Wood adds, "nature played a very big role. We really tried to use the elements: water, fire and earth. Water, the many places we see it. Untamed, unrestrained fire—which we see raging within the city of Asgard. We see it within the fire pots—the big flames, the choking flames.

"And just being in Iceland, shooting the plates, seeing the night skies, creating oceans in front of Asgard—again, it isn't tamed. It's rough."

Framestore concept art.

CHAPTER FOUR

BATTLE OF SVARTALFHEIM

One of the film's climactic battles takes place on the Dark Elves' devastated homeworld of Svartalfheim. The sons of Odin travel there together, reunited in a quest for justice and vengeance. But the events of *Thor* and *Marvel's The Avengers* have given Thor cause to doubt Loki's motives.

Executive Producer Craig Kyle cites the chemistry between actors Chris Hemsworth and Tom Hiddleston as a key to the sequence's success. "Some of my favorite scenes in the movie involve the two of them. They're the De Niro and Pacino of this film. Seeing them on-screen together is just so exciting. The history, the emotion, the skill they both have—they're all over every frame. When those two are together, it's magic."

Svartalfheim mirrors the interior conflict between Thor and Loki. Production Designer Charles Wood describes it as the "complete polar opposite" of the living, breathing realm of Vanaheim.

"We wanted to create a world where the Dark Elves' civilization once thrived, completely," Wood says. "Once they had a culture that existed, and was healthy. Now, in the storyline, they are being basically wiped out."

Creative Executive Eric Carroll adds, "We thought it was important this time around to show more of the Nine Realms. That's kind of what's fun about Thor, right? Iron Man can't necessarily have an adventure on Svartalfheim, but Thor can visit any number of amazing worlds and places."

VFX still.

The battle of Svartalfheim kicks off with a hair-raising journey between the realms, as Thor and his allies fly off to battle in an Asgardian skiff.

"A substantial amount of work went into the design of this craft," recalls Cumron Ashtiani, Art Director of Atomhawk Design. "We were given Viking longboats as a reference, but we needed to make it fly. The world of Thor blends myth, magic and sci-fi together, so we didn't want to just make a magical flying boat. We wanted its design to suggest it uses a technology of some kind to fly, but that technology is unlike human tech. It has typical Asgardian elegance.

"The skiff is a day-to-day Asgardian vehicle—a little like a taxi, I suppose. So we had to get the right balance of day-to-day wear and tear vs. impressive Asgardian scale and attention to detail.

"Asgard is often represented as bathed in golden sunlight, and it also contains a lot of flowing water. This scene has a lot of mist and spray given off by waterfalls, caught in the low-angled sunlight."

Atomhawk Design concept art.

BATTLE OF SVARTALFHEIM

ANIMATICS BY FEDERICO D'ALESSANDRO & RICK NEWSOME

After Thor and company arrive in Svartalfheim, Loki makes his move. According to Animatics Supervisor Federico D'Alessandro, the twists and turns of this sequence made it particularly tricky to pull off.

"Having worked on many of Marvel's movies, I've developed a strong and trusting relationship with the studio, and they graciously encourage me to take a strong creative role in their projects," D'Alessandro says. "Sometimes this means creating sequences practically from scratch, and other times it means identifying and solving story problems. But the common denominator is that every scene comes with its own unique challenges."

VFX still.

LOKI- This plan of yours...
...it's not going to work.
LOKI- But I want you to know...
LOKI- But I want you to know...
...that I've truly enjoyed our time together.

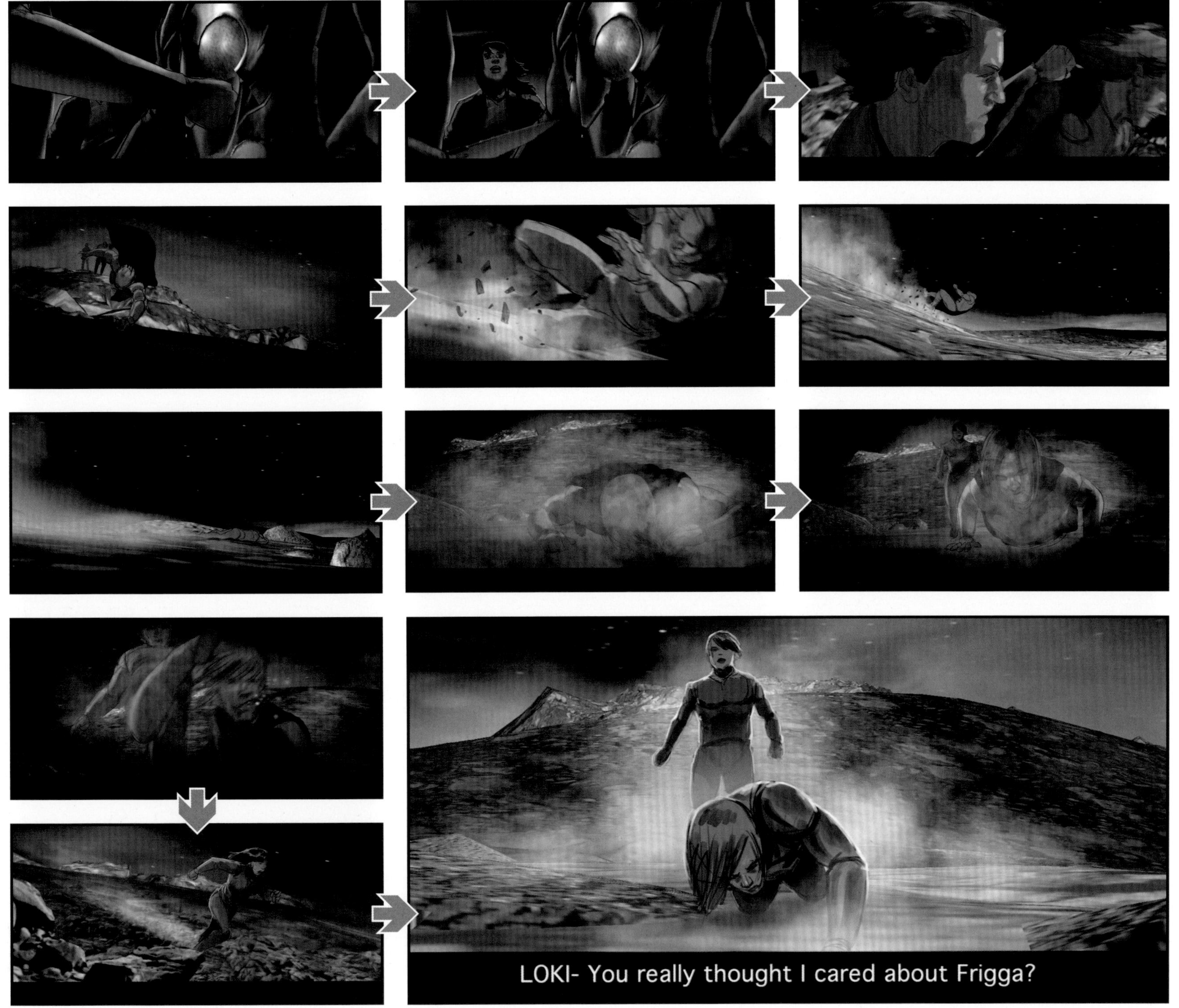
LOKI- You really thought I cared about Frigga?

"The plan begins with Loki stabbing Thor in the side, shoving him down the hill and kicking him viciously," D'Alessandro explains. "I amp up the tension with Jane scrambling down the slope, as well as the Dark Elves descending on them. A seriously wounded Thor reaches for his hammer—and as it flies towards him, Loki cements his betrayal by cutting Thor's hand off!"

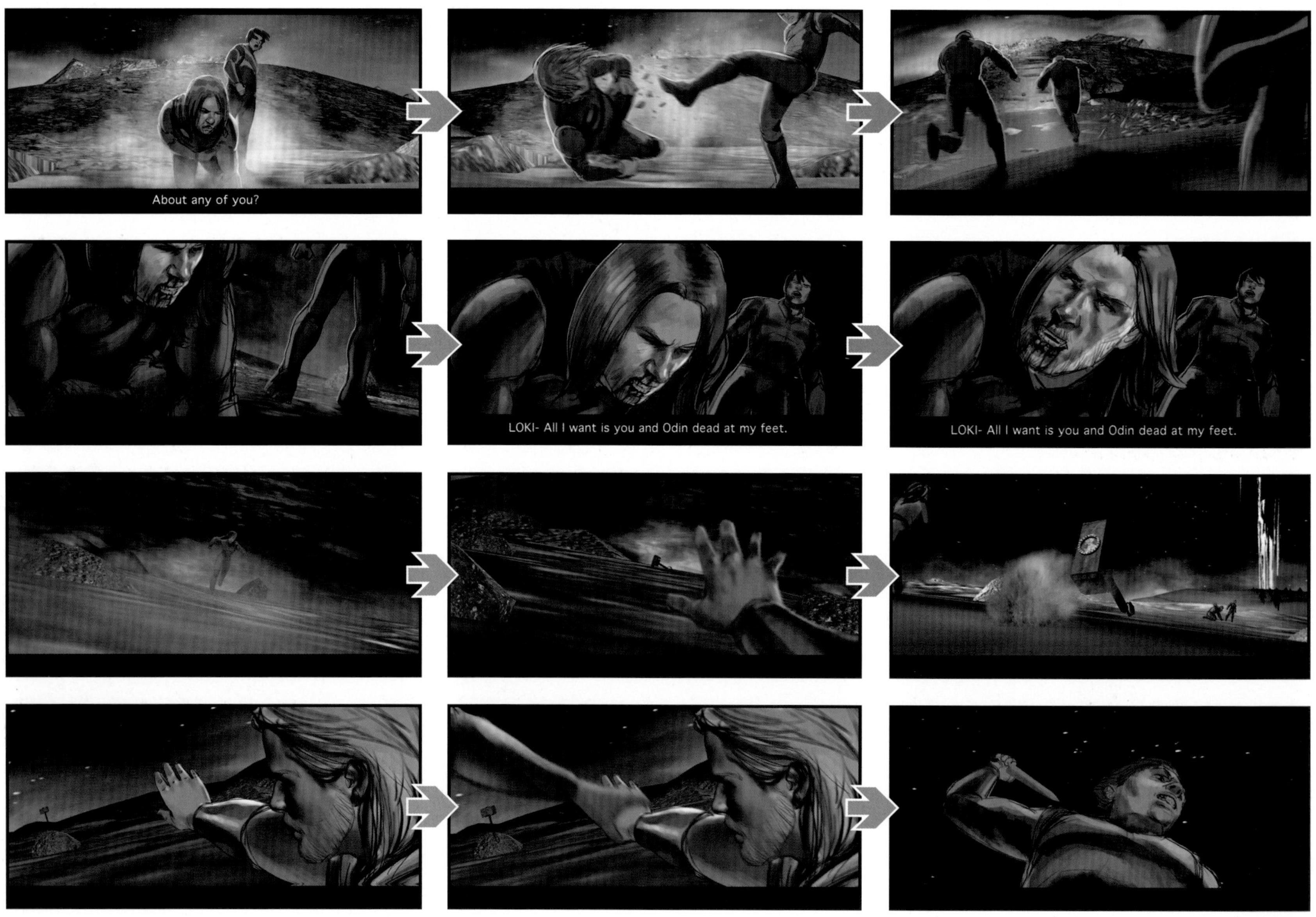

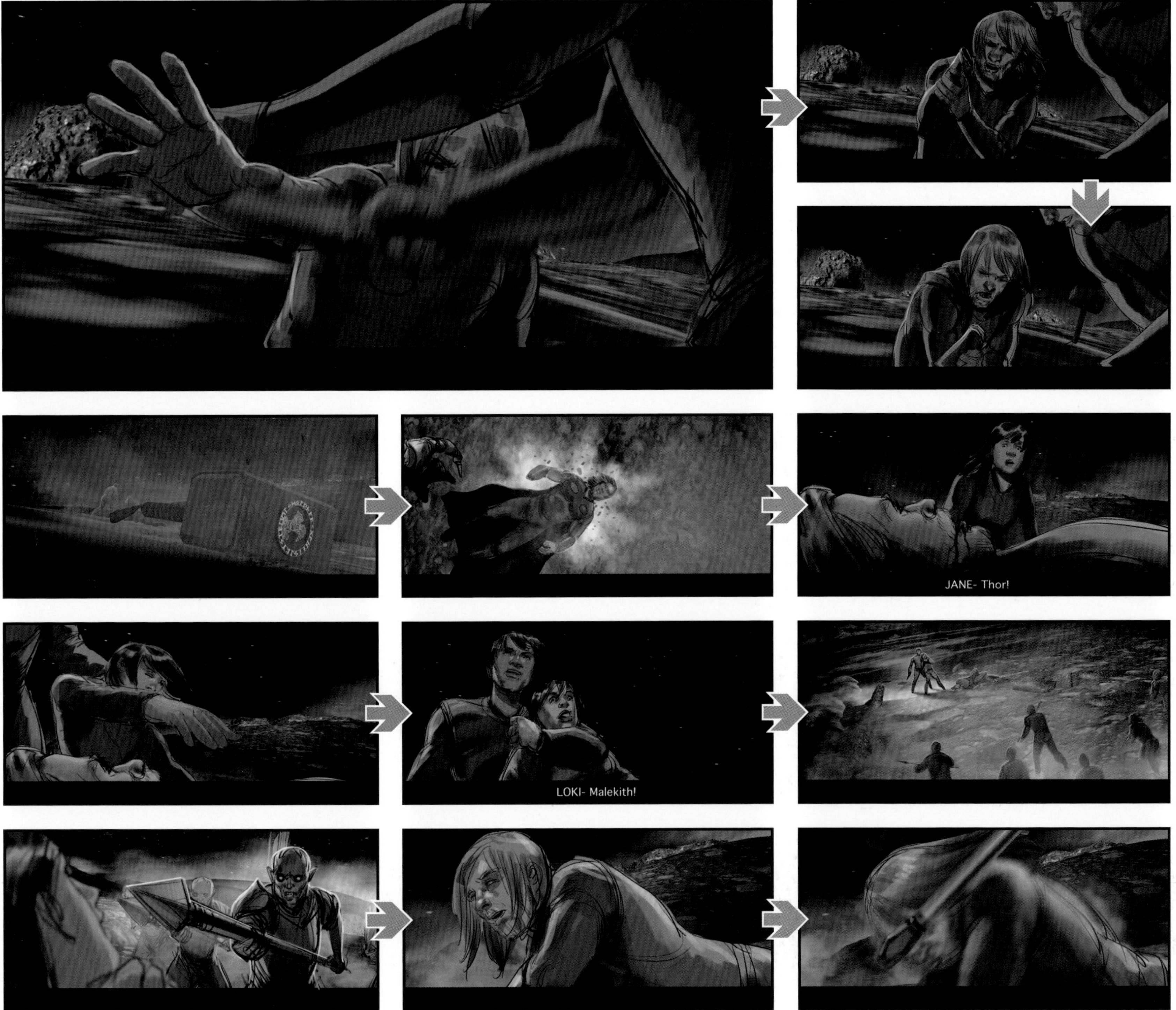
JANE- Thor!
LOKI- Malekith!

D'Alessandro: "I thought there was a chance my idea would be deemed too graphic to be included in the film, but decided to keep it in the animatic with the hope that the emotional impact of the moment could overcome any possible trepidation. Wanting to preserve the surprise, I kept the idea to myself so that Alan Taylor and Marvel had no clue it was coming when they saw the animatic for the first time. Thankfully, they really responded to the moment, and it stayed in the film."

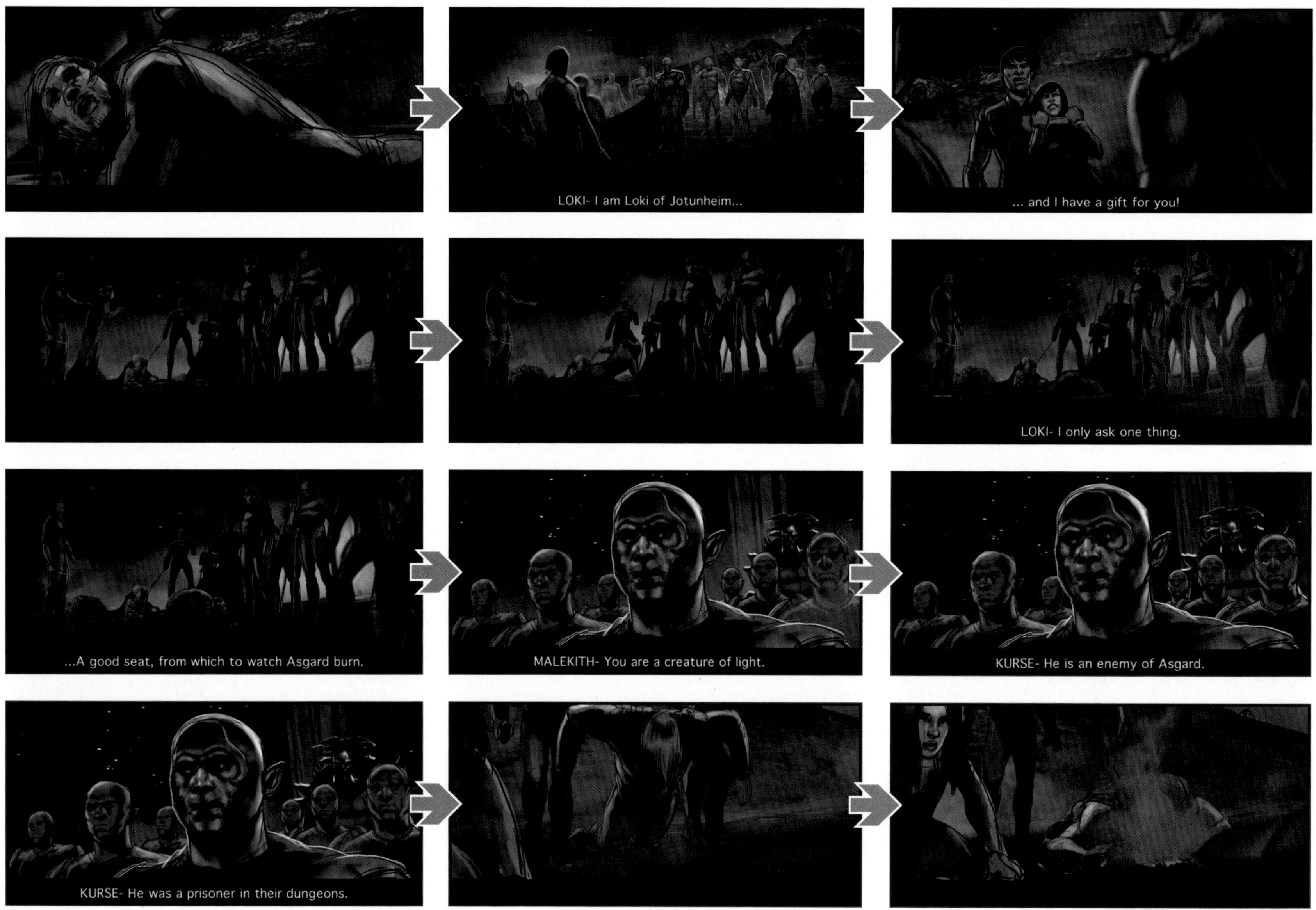

MALEKITH- Look at me!
MALEKITH- Thank you.

VFX still.

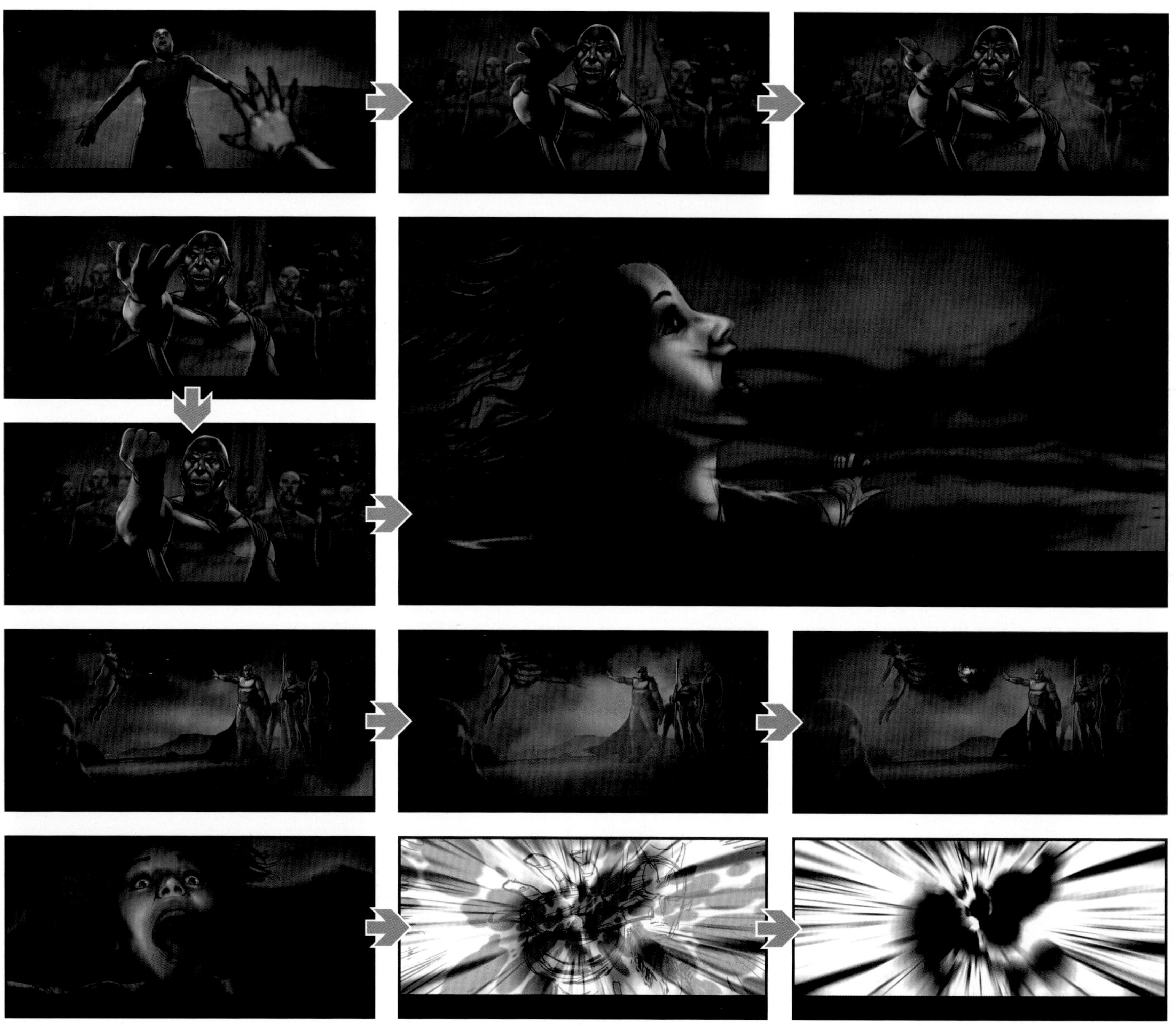

Storyboard Artist Rick Newsome contributed the middle section of this scene, in which Jane Foster witnesses a vision of universal cosmic destruction.

"This was one of the more challenging assignments on the film," Newsome says. "The script described dark energy spreading out across the Earth and through a network of wormholes, ultimately consuming the Nine Realms.

"That was a lot of ground to cover, and pretty abstract. So abstract, in fact, that the true horror of Jane's experience might be difficult to convey—so I made sure to add some people being consumed at the beginning. This was not mentioned specifically in the script, but it was important to anchor the calamity at a human scale before we went cosmic with the destruction."

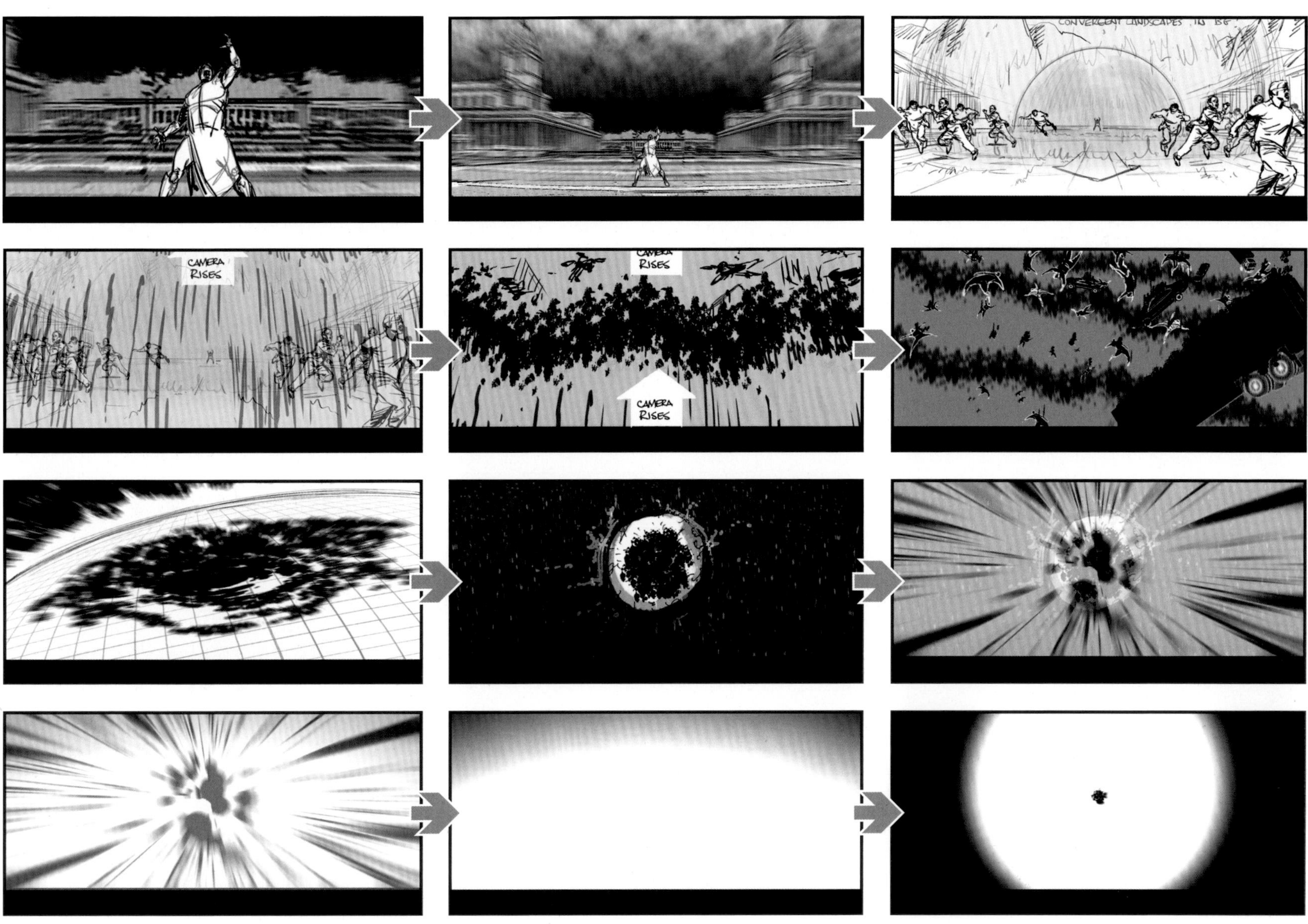

"The rest of the sequence amounted to a cosmic fly-through, transitioning from Earth as we know it to the multi-dimensionality of the Nine Realms," Newsome continues. "In the cosmology of Thor—as in Norse cosmology—the Nine Realms are contained or linked to a giant tree: Yggdrasil. The fly-through takes us into the roots of the tree as the darkness spreads, and then the shot widens as the entire tree goes black. Even if the audience doesn't recognize the significance of the tree, I hope the symbolism is clear: The light has gone out in the tree of life.

"I was inspired by something right in Marvel's own backyard, so to speak. A close viewing of the end titles of the first *Thor* movie depict what looks to me like a trip through the Nine Realms, including the roots and branches of Yggdrasil. I've never confirmed that this was the intention—but in any case, the images served as a starting point for my own depiction of the Thor cosmos."

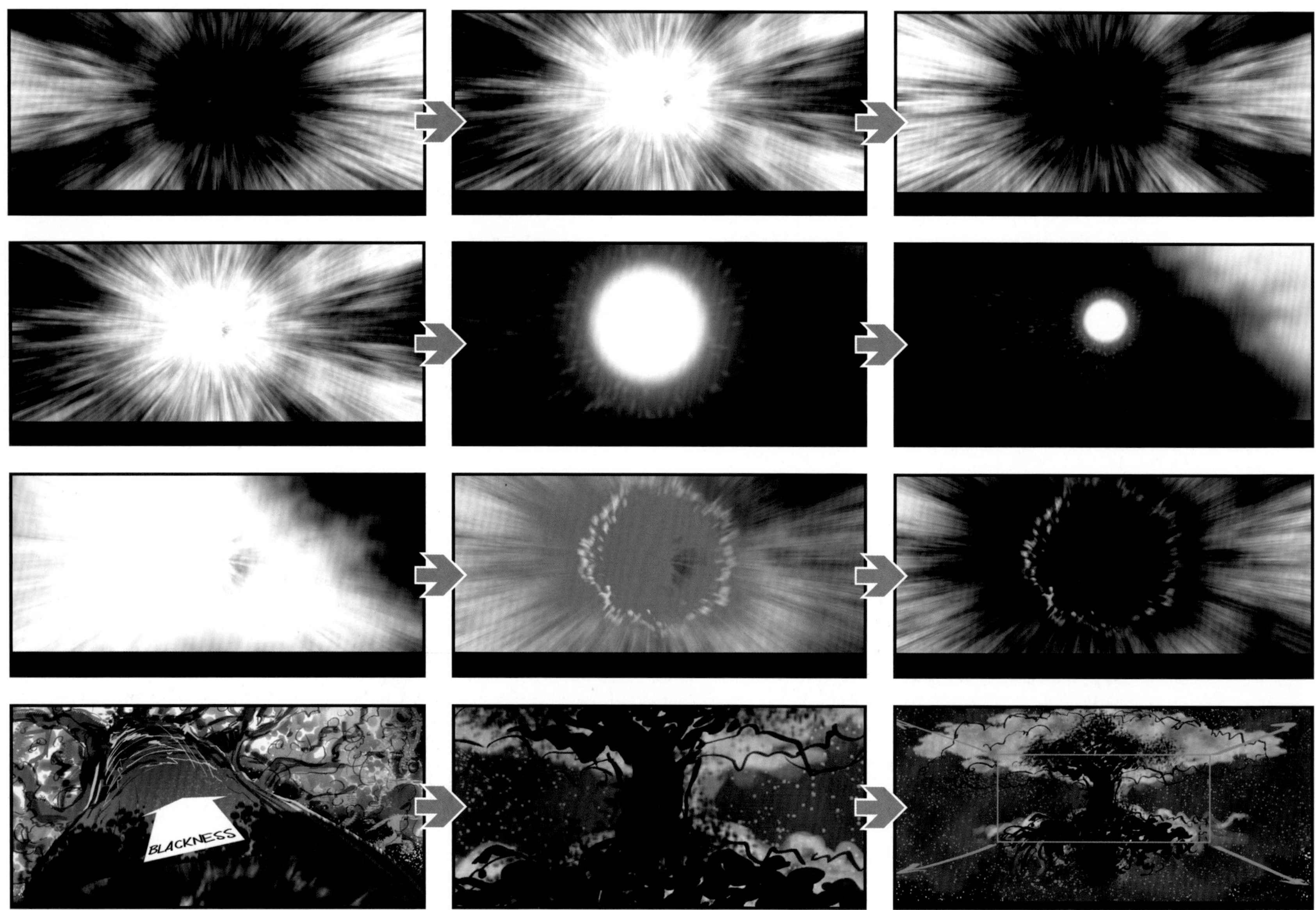

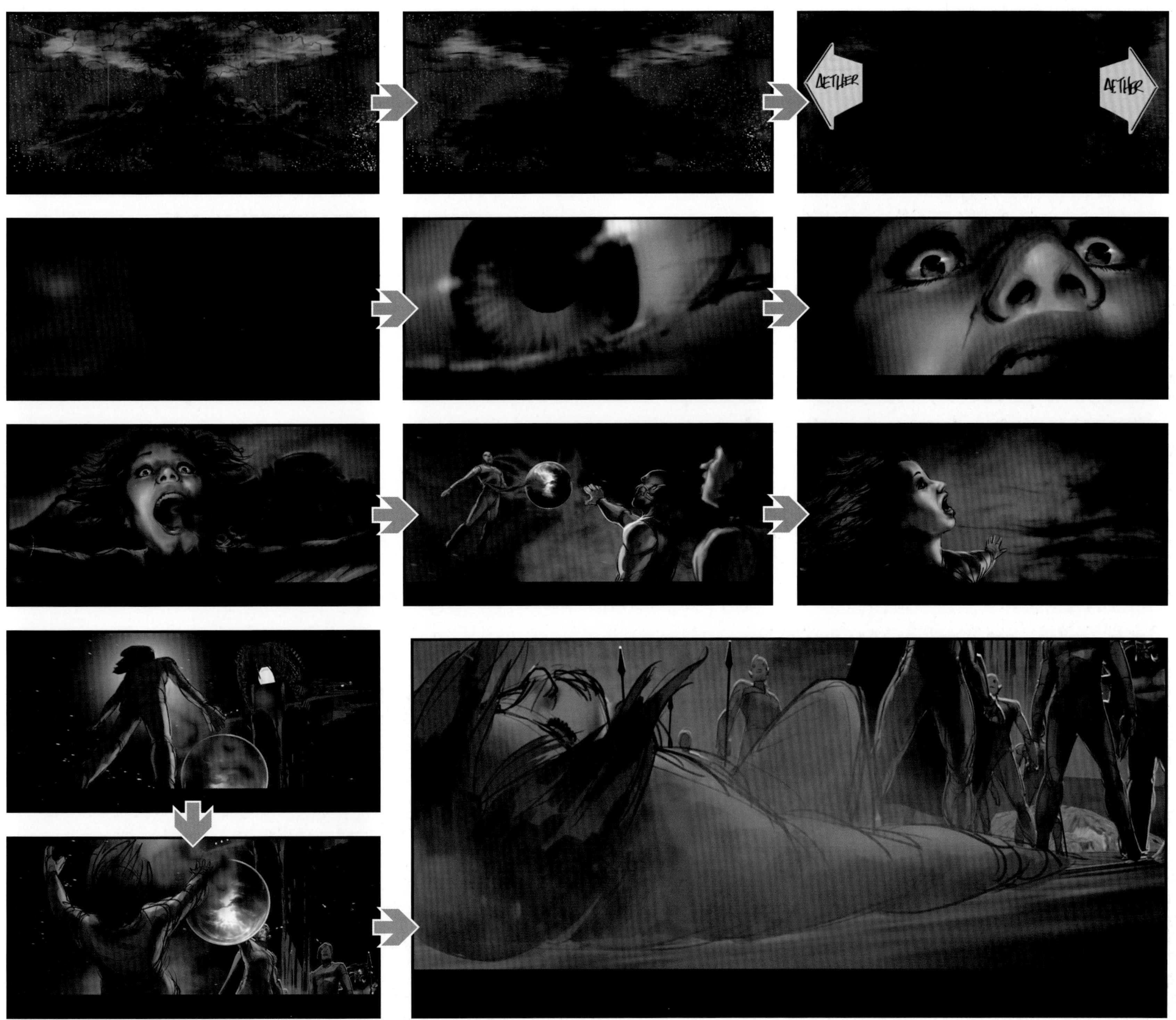
AETHER
AETHER

CHAPTER FIVE

MARKETING THOR: THE DARK WORLD

During the course of planning a film's promotion, dozens of ideas and sketches are produced. John Sabel, Executive Vice President of Motion Picture Creative Print Marketing for Walt Disney Studios, gives us a peek behind the scenes.

"What I love about the Marvel process and the way it's structured is that we meet real early on with Kevin Feige and Lou D'Esposito and the filmmakers, and we throw around ideas. We talk about the tone and about past campaigns and what we would like to see, and then we do a lot of sketches. And at the same time, we're thinking about what photographer would be perfect for this.

"Then we go back to our ad agency, BLT, and they do a bunch of sketches and come up with some stuff. We also talk about logos and try to set the groundwork and the feel for the campaign—whether we want to go darker or brighter, how do we want Thor to look, who else should be on the poster. Then we start doing the sketches, then we do a photo shoot. Then we start building all kinds of different comps and all the different directions that we'd talk about.

"And then we'll pin them all up and spread them all in a big room, and we all walk around and look. We make comments and we fine-tune them again, and then we come back and make another presentation. Usually, we nail it.

"BLT is a key component. I'm the creative director on it and work with Warren Young and my team over at Disney, and we guide it through. Really, what we're trying to do is make this feel like an epic movie, and we're trying to make it fun. We're trying to take that dark edge and put a little color in it, balancing between the comic-book world and the real world. It's a balance."

First theatrical teaser poster.

Loki character poster.

Limited-edition collectible poster by Charlie Wen, San Diego Comic-Con 2013.

Marvel Head of Visual Development Charlie Wen explains the origins of the iconic poster he created for Comic-Con 2013: "This piece actually started as a thumbnail when we were exploring ideas for the first film's poster. At that time I was trying to capture something pure, something that made a clear statement about who Thor really was. However, it was far too idealized, with some of the shapes, to reflect the tone and style of *Thor*.

"While brainstorming ideas for the SDCC 2013 poster, Craig Kyle sent me over the thumbnail for this image as a suggestion. I had always been very excited about this piece, as a fan of Thor myself, so I was eager to bring the image back. I added in the storm and the gusty winds blowing against him, to bring him into the world of *Thor: The Dark World*—a world that was much more based in reality.

"Kevin Feige felt that adding more of the characters from *Thor: The Dark World* would make the piece feel a bit more specific to the film, so I went in and added them after the original piece was finished."

"We do the San Diego Comic-Con collectible posters for the fans," John Sabel says. "The fans love it; we love it. Each one of these films is a special event, and those posters are collectible. They almost become trophies, a marker for the event. People collect the posters just like they collect comic books."

Production still.

AFTERWORD

Working on *Thor: The Dark World* was both an amazing experience and a unique challenge. As a sequel, the goal was to create spectacular and diverse worlds that were also credible and authentic, and built on what we saw in the very successful first film. Continuous shepherding from Marvel Studios and Director Alan Taylor helped our team develop a vast range of new ideas.

Always seeking to push the boundaries of design, we wanted to achieve a look that was rich in detail and fit for the gods. The initial design stages were critical, providing the backbone to the expansion of Thor, both as a Norse god and as a Marvel character.

Our aim was to find harmony between myth, fantasy and technology. The film needed to embrace a range of contrasts—from the blackened, broken tundra of Svartalfheim to the thriving, spectacular realm of Asgard.

To achieve this required an incredible crew. Highly talented illustrators and designers drew sets that could only be realized by expert construction crews. The skill and artistry of the sculptors, painters and plasterers who worked on *Thor: The Dark World* was unparalleled.

Supervising Art Director Ray Chan, Set Decorator John Bush and Construction Manager John Bohan were simply brilliant.

I also have to thank our exceptionally skilled art directors: Mike Stallion, Mark Swain, Tom Brown, Julian Ashby and Jordan Crockett.

In addition, creating these worlds would have been impossible without the support of the Visual Effects department, so ably led by Jake Morrison and his team.

Throughout the whole undertaking, I took great comfort in knowing that I had such a skilled team around me.

Above all, I'd like to thank the entire crew for their dedication to their work on *Thor: The Dark World*.

Charles Wood

Charles Wood
2011

Director **Alan Taylor** came to his career in film and television by a roundabout route. Raised in Canada, Taylor moved to New York City to study European history at Columbia University, but changed course two years into the PhD program and entered the film program at NYU. His graduate thesis film, *That Burning Question*, earned multiple awards and launched his career. He followed several episodes of *Homicide: Life on the Street* with his first feature, the award-winning *Palookaville*. That New Jersey-set heist comedy was seen by David Chase, who invited Taylor to join the creative team of HBO's hit series *The Sopranos*. Taylor went on to direct multiple episodes, winning an Emmy for "Heidi and Kennedy." Two more indie features followed: *The Emperor's New Clothes*, an award-winning adaptation of Simon Leys' fanciful novel retelling Napoleon's final days; and *Kill the Poor*, based on Joel Rose's comic but incendiary novel set in New York's Lower East Side during the 1980s. Taylor continued to work in television, earning acclaim on some of the most highly respected cable and network shows: *Sex and the City, Carnivale, Six Feet Under, Rome, Bored to Death, Boardwalk Empire, West Wing* and *Lost*. He received two further Emmy nominations and won the Director's Guild award for the pilot of AMC's *Mad Men*. In 2011, Taylor directed the final two episodes of *Game of Thrones*' freshman season. He then joined *GOT* as executive producer for season two, directing four more episodes and garnering his third Emmy nomination.

Producer and Marvel Studios President **Kevin Feige** has guided the studio through more than a decade of films and was instrumental in starting up the current era of movies produced directly by the studio. Feige serves as producer for the studio's entire slate of films—including *Iron Man, Iron Man 2, The Incredible Hulk, Thor, Captain America: The First Avenger, Marvel's The Avengers, Iron Man 3* and *Thor: The Dark World*, as well as the upcoming *Captain America: The Winter Soldier, Guardians of the Galaxy, The Avengers: Age of Ultron* and *Ant-Man*. In that role, it falls to him to coordinate the emergent Marvel Cinematic Universe between the different productions—drawing together a talented pool of directors, producers, actors and artists to create a coherent film world, the likes of which Hollywood has never attempted. Since joining Marvel in 2000, Feige has been involved in key capacities for all of the company's theatrical film productions. He served as executive producer on the second and third *Spider-Man* films, co-produced *X2: X-Men United*, and executive produced *X-Men 3: The Last Stand*. Feige was named Motion Picture Showman of the Year for 2012 by the Publicists of the International Cinematographers Guild.

Executive Producer and Marvel Studios Co-President **Louis D'Esposito** served as Executive Producer on the blockbuster hits *Iron Man, Iron Man 2, Thor, Captain America: The First Avenger, Marvel's The Avengers* and *Iron Man 3*. He is also currently working on *Captain America: The Winter Soldier* and *Guardians of the Galaxy* as well as working with Marvel Studios President Kevin Feige to build the future Marvel slate. As Co-President of the studio and Executive Producer on all Marvel films, D'Esposito balances running the studio to overseeing each film from its development stage to distribution. Beyond his role as Co-President of Marvel Studios, D'Esposito is also directing unique filmed projects for the

studio including his one-shot titled *Agent Carter* starring Hayley Atwell that debuted at the 2013 Comic-Con International in San Diego. D'Esposito also directed the short film titled *Item 47* for Marvel, which made its debut to fans at the 2012 Comic-Con International in San Diego and was featured again at the LA Shorts Fest in September 2012. The project was released as an added feature on *Marvel's The Avengers* Blu-ray disc. D'Esposito began his tenure at Marvel Studios in 2006. Prior to Marvel, D'Esposito's executive producing credits include the 2006 hit film *The Pursuit of Happyness* starring Will Smith, *Zathura: A Space Adventure* and the 2003 hit *S.W.A.T.* starring Samuel L. Jackson and Colin Farrell.

Executive Producer **Victoria Alonso** is currently executive producing Alan Taylor's *Thor: The Dark World*, Joe and Anthony Russo's *Captain America: The Winter Soldier* and James Gunn's *Guardians of the Galaxy* for Marvel Studios, where she serves as Executive Vice President of Visual Effects and Post Production. She executive produced Shane Black's *Iron Man 3* as well as *Marvel's The Avengers* for writer/director Joss Whedon and co-produced *Iron Man* and *Iron Man 2* with director Jon Favreau, Kenneth Branagh's *Thor* and Joe Johnston's *Captain America: The First Avenger*. Alonso's career began at the nascency of the visual effects industry, when she served as a commercial VFX producer. From there, she VFX-produced numerous feature films, working with such directors as Ridley Scott (*Kingdom of Heaven*), Tim Burton (*Big Fish*) and Andrew Adamson (*Shrek*), to name a few.

Thor Executive Producer **Craig Kyle** began his career at Marvel Studios in 2001 as the sole Creative Executive for the company's animation division. He has developed, produced and written numerous animated series, and oversaw the development and production of Marvel's original animated direct-to-DVD projects—including *Ultimate Avengers, Ultimate Avengers II, Invincible Iron Man, Hulk Vs., Next Avengers, Doctor Strange, Planet Hulk* and *Thor: Tales of Asgard*. Five years ago, Kyle was promoted to SVP of Production and Development of Marvel Studios' live-action division, where he produced *Thor*.

Executive Producer **Nigel Gostelow** came to movie-making straight from school at the tender age of 18. He started as a "gofer" on movies such as *Krull, Superman III* and *Supergirl* before graduating to 3rd Assistant Director for *Spies Like Us* and *Santa Claus: The Movie*. After a long spell as Location Manager, Gostelow settled into the role of Unit Production Manager—first for HBO, and then on John Madden's *Captain Corelli's Mandolin*, Christopher Nolan's *Batman Begins* and Paul Greengrass' *The Bourne Ultimatum*, among others—before serving as Executive Producer on Joe Johnston's *The Wolfman* and *Captain America: The First Avenger*. Gostelow also executive produced Tim Burton's *Dark Shadows* before returning to Marvel for Alan Taylor's *Thor: The Dark World*. He is executive producing a new movie, to be filmed in 2014. Gostelow lives with his family in the UK and spends some of his spare time keeping a number of old cars road-worthy.

Jackson Sze keyframe.

Production Designer **Charles Wood** began his entertainment-industry career in 1991 as a Visual Effects Art Director on such projects as *The Fugitive*, Peter Weir's *Fearless*, *Under Siege* and Sam Raimi's *Army of Darkness*. Segueing to design work, he has since collaborated on projects ranging from big studio movies to independent films. His credits include *Thor: The Dark World*, Joe Carnahan's *The A-Team*, Michael Apted's *Amazing Grace*, *Wrath of the Titans*, *Fool's Gold*, Tony Bill's *Flyboys*, F. Gary Gray's *The Italian Job*, *Get Carter* and *Mortal Kombat: Annihilation*. Charles is currently working on Marvel's *Guardians of the Galaxy*. Wood earned an Emmy Award nomination in 2000 for the TV movie *Geppetto* and a 2007 Satellite Award nomination for *Amazing Grace*.

Costume Designer **Wendy Partridge** has built a distinguished career designing costumes for both feature films and television, most recently on *Thor: The Dark World* and *Resident Evil: Retribution*. Among her numerous other credits are *Hellboy*, for which she was nominated for a Saturn Award for Best Costumes, *Conan the Barbarian*, *Legion*, *Resurrecting the Champ*, *Silent Hill*, *Fantastic 4*, *Underworld*, *Underworld: Evolution*, *The Hitcher II: I've Been Waiting*, *Blade II*, *Texas Rangers*, *Snow Day*, *Whiteout* and *Highlander: Endgame*. In 2008, she was nominated for an Emmy Award for Outstanding Costumes for her work on the TV movie *Broken Trail*. In 2013, for the inaugural Canadian Screen and Television Awards, she received a record three nominations for her work on *Resident Evil: Retribution*, *Silent Hill* and *Hannah's Law*. Partridge garnered Canadian Genie Awards for her work on the features *Passchendaele* (2009) and *Loyalties* (1987), and received Genie nominations for her costume designs on *Come l'America*, *Isaac Littlefeathers* and *Latitude 55*. Partridge's television credits include AMC's *Hell on Wheels*, *The Secret of the Nutcracker*, *Ultra*, *Call Me: The Rise and Fall of Heidi Fleiss*, *High Noon*, *Heart Full of Rain*, *In Cold Blood* and the series *Lonesome Dove: The Outlaw Years*.

Director of Photography **Kramer Morgenthau ASC** has traveled the globe shooting more than 20 feature films and numerous TV, documentary and commercial assignments. His recent feature projects include *Chef* with director Jon Favreau, *Feast of Love* with three-time Academy Award-winning director Robert Benton and *Fracture* with director Gregory Hoblit. In the world of television, Morgenthau has been nominated for five Emmy Awards and four ASC Awards. He recently shot *Game of Thrones* (HBO), for which he won an Outstanding Achievement Award in Cinematography from the American Society of Cinematographers. He also shot and was nominated for Emmy Awards for *Boardwalk Empire* (HBO), *Too Big to Fail* (HBO), *FlashForward* (ABC), and *Life on Mars* (ABC). In 2011, Morgenthau was named one of 10 Cinematographers to watch by *Variety* magazine. In August 2013, he was featured in *Variety*'s Below the Line Impact report. Morgenthau has worked with a wide range of directors and began his career shooting documentaries based out of New York City.

Marvel Head of Visual Development **Charlie Wen** has held a variety of positions in the entertainment industry, ranging from concept designer to art director, on everything from feature films to video games and animation. Wen's client list reads as a virtual who's who of the industry, including Disney, Digital Domain, Dreamworks, Legendary Pictures, Marvel Studios, Darkhorse, Rhythm and Hues, Imagi Studios, Wizards of the Coast and Sony Computer Entertainment of America. In 2005, he created Kratos and helped establish *God of War* as a monolithic action-adventure title for Sony PlayStation. Outside the production environment, Wen has given lectures on figure drawing and character design at many distinguished studios and universities. After helping establish the main character designs in *Thor*, he holds the title of Head of Visual Development at Marvel Studios, working on *Captain America: The First Avenger*, *Marvel's The Avengers*, *Iron Man 3*, *Thor: The Dark World*, *Guardians of the Galaxy*, *Captain America: The Winter Soldier* and *The Avengers: Age of Ultron*.

Special Makeup Effects/Prosthetics Designer **David White** began his career at age 19 as an assistant to Makeup Effects Artist Nick Maley on *The Keep* (1982). White went on to work for Creature Effects Designer Lyle Conway on *Return to Oz* (1983) as a sculptor, and again for Maley on *Lifeforce* (1984). White joined the Makeup Effects team on *Little Shop of Horrors* (1985) as Senior Painter and Animatronics Technician of the Audrey II plants. Following his work on Mary Shelley's *Frankenstein* (1994) as a Makeup Effects Designer, White formed his own company, Altered States FX, with business partner Sacha Carter. Based at Shepperton Studios, White oversaw all prosthetic work from design to final on-set application on many projects. He received his first Emmy Award nomination for the TNT movie *The Hunchback*; his prosthetic design work on Robbie Williams in the music video for "Rock DJ" became a multi-award winner in the Best Special Effects category. He worked on Ridley Scott's *Kingdom of Heaven* and Tony Scott's *Spy Game*, also creating prosthetics for films such as *The Da Vinci Code*, *La Vie en Rose* and *In Bruges*. He subsequently served as head of department on films such as Ridley Scott's *Robin Hood*, Joe Johnston's *Captain America: The First Avenger* and *Snow White and the Huntsman*. His most recent credits as Special Makeup Designer include Disney's *Maleficent* and Marvel's *Thor: The Dark World*. White is heading up the Special Makeup Effects department on one of Marvel's latest movies, *Guardians of the Galaxy*.

Property Master **Barry Gibbs** has worked in film since 1981, when he started his career as a stagehand with Model Units on *Krull* and *Supergirl*, with The Rank Organisation at Pinewood Studios. He shortly moved to Props, where his first jobs included Ridley Scott's *Legend* and the Bond film *A View To A Kill*. Gibbs gained experience in the disciplines of set dressing and standing by on set, then went freelance in 1985 with Julien Temple's *Absolute Beginners*. Three years later, he had the first offer of a Prop Master position on *Roald Dahl's Danny the Champion of the World*. At that time, he split his efforts between feature films and commercials. This continued until 1993, when Gibbs went to Ireland for *Circle of Friends* with Production Designer Jim Clay. Since then, he has worked on *Captain Correlli's Mandolin*, *About a Boy*, *Love Actually*, *Timeline*, *The Golden Compass*, *Quantum of Solace* and *Inception* among others. Gibbs' avid interest in manufacturing keeps him involved with and running large prop shops with amazing teams of technicians. He was given the opportunity to work for Marvel on *Captain America: The First Avenger* and continued with the studio to help produce *Thor: The Dark World* and the upcoming *Guardians of the Galaxy*. His motivation and desire to continue ensuring delivery of high-quality props has worn off on his family, with his wife Hayley joining him in Props and their daughter Lily gaining experience in the Costume Department.

Set Decorator **John Bush** started his career in theater and then moved to BBC Television, where he worked for 15 years as a Props Buyer and Set Dresser on major TV dramas, and light entertainment and arts programs. Since leaving the BBC, he has spent 20 years as a freelance Set Decorator on more than 30 films—including Mike Leigh's *Topsy-Turvy* and *Vera Drake*, Terence Davies' *House of Mirth*, comedies such as *About a Boy* and *Johnny English*, Steven Spielberg's *Munich*, Tim Burton's *Dark Shadows*, and *Captain America: The First Avenger* for Marvel Studios. He has been nominated for an Oscar and other awards, and has won an Emmy. He lives in London and keeps in touch with his professional roots by occasionally designing sets for his local theater group.

Visual Effects Supervisor **Jake Morrison** has been blending photography and computer graphics for more than 20 years. Pursuing an early interest in creating real-time visuals to be performed alongside live music, Morrison taught himself a programming language and learned video-sampling techniques. This led to a career that encompassed commercials, television and, for the last 16 years, film. Working on the VFX-vendor side, Morrison served as VFX/CG Supervisor and Lead Compositor on many projects—including Peter Jackson's *The Lord of the Rings: The Two Towers*, and the Wachowski's *The Matrix Reloaded* and *The Matrix Revolutions*—before crossing over to the production side with Digital Effects Supervisor credits on Warner Bros' *300* for Zack Snyder and the Wachowski's *Speed Racer*. Morrison has been working with Marvel Studios, providing Additional VFX Supervision on Kenneth Branagh's *Thor* and serving as 2nd Unit VFX Supervisor on Joss Whedon's *Marvel's The Avengers*.

Concept Artist **Andy Park** began his career illustrating comic books for about a decade on titles such as *Tomb Raider*, *Excalibur* and *Uncanny X-Men* for companies like Marvel, DC and Image Comics. In 2004, he began working as a concept artist in video games and television. He was one of the lead artists creating the worlds and characters of the award-winning *God of War* franchise for Sony Computer Entertainment of America. Park has since joined the team at Marvel Studios as a Visual Development illustrator, designing characters and keyframes for *Marvel's The Avengers*, *Captain America: The First Avenger* and *Iron Man 3*, as well as the upcoming *Guardians of the Galaxy*, *Captain America: The Winter Soldier* and *The Avengers: Age of Ultron*.

Concept Artist **Jackson Sze** has worked in advertising, video games, television and film for studios such as Lucasfilm Animation and Sony Computer Entertainment of America. He is a founding member of the BATTLEMiLK series of art books and is a Senior Concept Illustrator at Marvel Studios. His projects include *Marvel's The Avengers*, *Guardians of the Galaxy* and *Ant-Man*.

Animatics Supervisor **Federico D'Alessandro** was born in Uruguay and raised in Colorado. He has made a name for himself as one of the top storyboard artists in Hollywood and was a key creative force behind a multitude of blockbuster films including *I Am Legend*, *Where the Wild Things Are* and *The Chronicles of Narnia* series. Since joining Marvel Studios in 2009, he has played an important creative role in films such as *Thor*, *Captain America: The First Avenger*, *Marvel's The Avengers*, *Iron Man 3*, *Captain America: The Winter Soldier*, *Thor: The Dark World* and the upcoming *The Avengers: Age of Ultron*.

Storyboard Artist **Bryan Andrews**, known in the industry for his uncanny ability to board scenes of high drama with uniquely inspiring takes on action storytelling, has been impressing science-fiction action fans for almost a decade since his Emmy Award-winning contributions to animated series *Star Wars: Clone Wars* and *Samurai Jack*. He also co-created *Sym-Bionic Titan*. Citing influences that range from Steven Spielberg, Ray Harryhausen and Akira Kurosawa to Frank Frazetta, Gatchaman and Macross—and an avid student of not only the visual language of cinema but also rapier fencing and Chinese martial arts such as Wushu and Wing Chun—Andrews has brought his trademark flair for dramatic action storytelling to both the small and silver screens. He attended Cal Arts in Valencia, California, and has worked on *Iron Man 2*, *Marvel's The Avengers* and *Thor: The Dark World*.

Storyboard Artist **Jane Wu** finds that storyboarding is the perfect expression of her passion and talent for storytelling and action. A native of Taiwan, Wu studied Wushu, where she developed the ability to choreograph the dynamic action sequences that have made her one of the "go to" story artists for action. She further honed her artistry through the study of fashion and costume design at Otis Parson's School of Art and Design, where she taught for many years. Wu has boarded or directed animated shows including *Men in Black*, *Jackie Chan Adventures* and *Tinkerbell*. She has boarded on numerous live-action films including *The A-Team*, *Percy Jackson: Sea of Monsters* and *Marvel's The Avengers*. As a woman boarding on action films, Wu offers a distinctive point of view and proudly occupies a unique place in the movie business.

Storyboard Artist **Rick Newsome**'s early enthusiasm for both drawing and film led him to a career as a storyboard artist in the motion picture industry. In addition to *Thor: The Dark World*, his long list of credits includes many popular films such as *Titanic*, *Independence Day*, *X2: X-Men United*, *Spider-Man 3*, *The Incredible Hulk*, *Alice in Wonderland* and *Argo*. A lifelong resident of southern California, he makes his home in Los Angeles.

All Bios 2011

Jackson Sze keyframe.

ACKNOWL

Jaimie Alexander
Victoria Alonso
Richard Anderson
Bryan Andrews
Tadanobu Asano
Cumron Ashtiani
Atomhawk Design
BLT & Associates
Blur Studios
Jennifer Bowes
John Bush
Eric Carroll
Paul Catling
Bob Cheshire
Vince Colletta
Darby Connor
Ben Cooke
Paul Corbould
Coral D'Alessandro
Federico D'Alessandro
Louis D'Esposito
Kat Dennings
Double Negative
Hayley Easton-Street
Christopher Eccleston
Idris Elba
Jools Faiers
Kevin Feige
Framestore
Anthony Francisco
Barry Gibbs
Nigel Gostelow
Chris Hemsworth
Tom Hiddleston
Anthony Hopkins
Andrew Hunt
Kevin Jenkins
Jacob Johnston
Andrew Kim
Jack Kirby

Magdalena Kusowska
Theodore W. Kutt
Craig Kyle
Stan Lee
Zachary Levi
Steve Markowski
J. McCoy
Matt Milla
Kramer Morgenthau
Jake Morrison

Rick Newsome
Josh Nizzi
Cyrille Nomberg
Steve Oliff
Dominique Pace
Andy Park
Wendy Partridge
Emma Pill
Natalie Portman
Gerardo Ramirez

Martin Rezard
Rene Russo
John Sabel
Nathan Schroeder
Constantine Sekeris
Walter Simonson
Ray Stevenson
Justin Sweet
Jackson Sze
Alan Taylor

The Third Floor
Frank Victoria
Dan Walker
Charlie Wen
David White
Tom Whitehouse
Carl Wilson
Charles Wood
Jane Wu
Christopher Yost
Warren Young

Richard Anderson
142-143, 146, 200-202

Atomhawk Design
60-67, 110-113, 210-211, 217-218, 220-221, 242-243

Blur Studios
102

Paul Catling
68-69, 114

Bob Cheshire
124-127, 148-149, 164-169, 174-179, 182-183, 186-187, 190-191, 206-207

Federico D'Alessandro
245-254, 257

Jools Faiers
1, 21, 272, Cover, Gatefold

Framestore
11, 32-37, 108, 116-121, 138-146, 152-153, 194-202, 236-239

Anthony Francisco
107

Kevin Jenkins
35-37, 118-121, 142-143, 146, 236-237

Magdalena Kusowska
128-131

Steve Markowski
54-56, 58-59

J. McCoy
32-33, 144-145, 152-153, 196-199

Rick Newsome
54-56, 58-59, 132-137, 254-257

Josh Nizzi
43

Cyrille Nomberg
156-161

Andy Park
4-5, 24, 30, 38-39, 52, 56-57, 72-73, 75, 77-78, 82-84, 86, 90-91, 93-95, 97, 103

Nathan Schroeder
122-123, 204-205, 208-209

Constantine Sekeris
192

Justin Sweet
42-45, 72, 74, 77-79, 92-95, 100

Jackson Sze
6-7, 26, 28, 39, 40-42, 44, 121, 150-151, 162, 170, 180-181, 222-223, 234-235, 264-267

The Third Floor
212-216, 219

Frank Victoria
171

Dan Walker
104-106, 109

Charlie Wen
8-9, 16-19, 50-51, 73-76, 79-80, 82, 86-88, 92-93, 95-100, 172, 184-185, 188, 261

Tom Whitehouse
106

Carl Wilson
170

Jane Wu
224-231, 233

MARVEL STUDIOS PRESENTS CHRIS HEMSWORTH NATALIE PORTMAN TOM HIDDLESTON AND ANTHONY HOPKINS AS ODIN "THOR: THE DARK WORLD" STELLAN SKARSGÅRD IDRIS ELBA CHRISTOPHER ECCLESTON ADEWALE AKINNUOYE-AGBAJE KAT DENNINGS RAY STEVENSON ZACHARY LEVI TADANOBU ASANO JAIMIE ALEXANDER WITH RENE RUSSO CASTING BY SARAH HALLEY FINN, C.S.A. MUSIC BY BRIAN TYLER MUSIC SUPERVISOR DAVE JORDAN VISUAL EFFECTS SUPERVISOR JAKE MORRISON COSTUME DESIGNER WENDY PARTRIDGE EDITED BY DAN LEBENTAL, A.C.E. WYATT SMITH PRODUCTION DESIGN CHARLES WOOD DIRECTOR OF PHOTOGRAPHY KRAMER MORGENTHAU, ASC EXECUTIVE PRODUCERS NIGEL GOSTELOW STAN LEE EXECUTIVE PRODUCER ALAN FINE EXECUTIVE PRODUCERS VICTORIA ALONSO CRAIG KYLE EXECUTIVE PRODUCER LOUIS D'ESPOSITO PRODUCED BY KEVIN FEIGE, p.g.a. STORY BY DON PAYNE AND ROBERT RODAT SCREENPLAY BY CHRISTOPHER L. YOST AND CHRISTOPHER MARKUS & STEPHEN McFEELY DIRECTED BY ALAN TAYLOR

MARVEL

Marvel.com/Thor

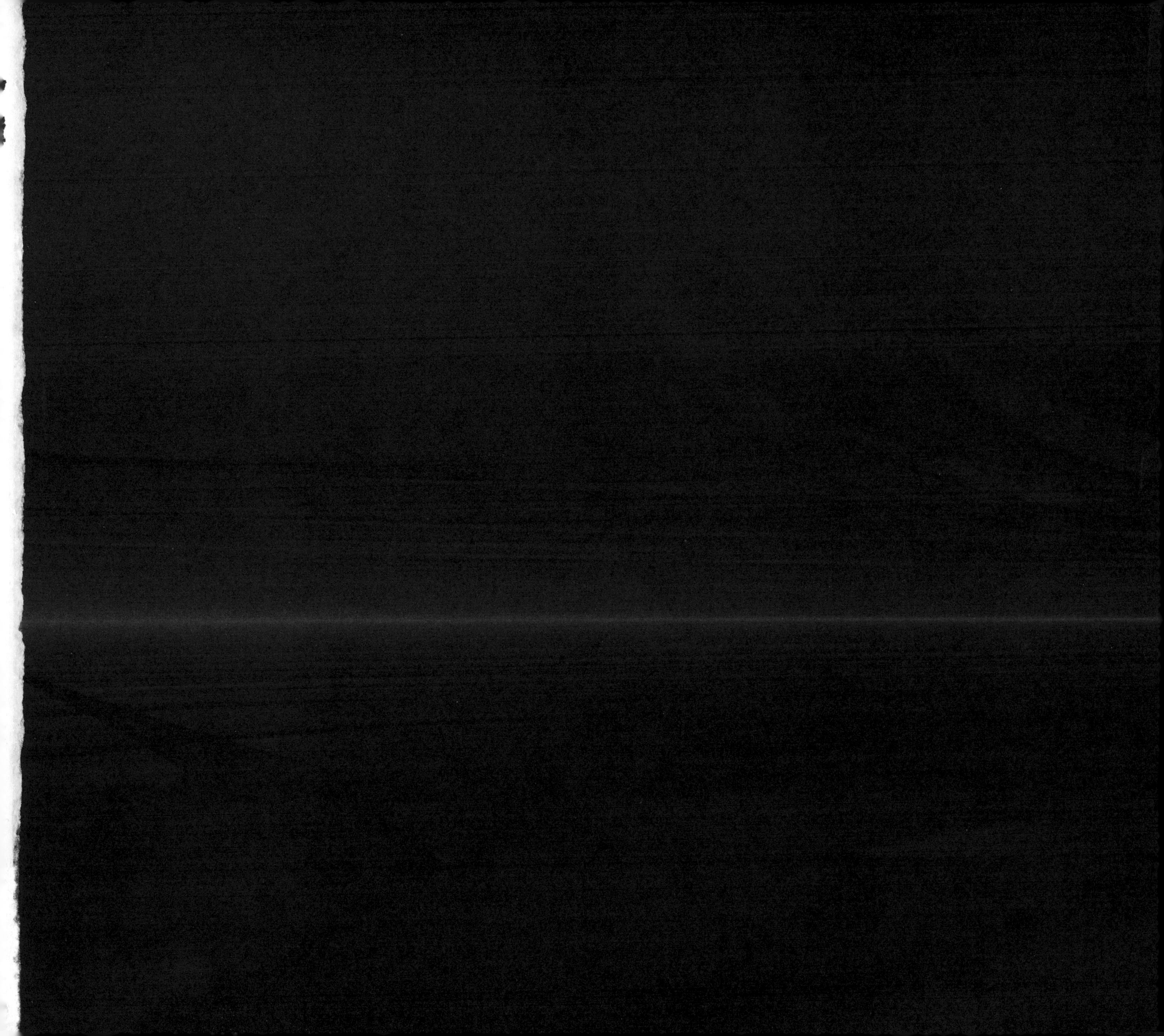